FASCINATING FACTS ABOUT LOVE, SEX & MARRIAGE

Albrecht Dürer, *Adam and Eve*.

RUTH BIRNKRANT

FASCINATING FACTS ABOUT LOVE, SEX & MARRIAGE

CROWN PUBLISHERS, INC.   NEW YORK

All illustrations are from the collection of Marion P. Geisinger, except for the following:
Andrew W. Mellon Fund, National Gallery of Art, Washington, D.C. (page 99); Bildarchiv Preussischer Kulturbesitz, West Berlin (page 119); British Library, London (page 108); British Museum, London (page 66); Condé Museum, Chantilly, France (page 10); Count Panza Di Biumo Collection/Leo Castelli Archives, New York (page 43); Corer Museum, Venice (page 65); Culver Pictures, New York (page 3); Solomon R. Guggenheim Museum, New York (pages 21, 126 top); *Gulliver's Travels*, illustrated by L. Rhead, Harper & Bros., New York & London, ca. 1913 (page 31); Rutherford B. Hayes Library, Fremont, Ohio (page 154 left and right); Ladies' Hermitage Association, Hermitage, Tennessee (page 143); Lion Country Safari, Laguna Hills, California (page 150); Louvre/Musées Nationaux, Paris (pages 20, 89, 173); Cartoon by Sir David Low by permission of the Low Trustees & the *Evening Standard,* London (page 85); Metropolitan Museum of Art/Gift of Paul J. Sachs, 1916 (page 129); Miami Beach News Service, Miami (page 87); Musée de Cluny/Musées Nationaux, Paris (page 127); Museum of Fine Arts, Boston (page 19); Museum of Man, Paris (page 40 right); National Library of Medicine, Bethesda, Maryland (pages 33, 120, 149); National Portrait Gallery, London (page 135 top right and left bottom); New-York Historical Society, New York (page 53); Spencer Museum of Art, The University of Kansas, Lawrence, Kansas (page 96); Franklin D. Roosevelt Library, Hyde Park, New York (pages 111, 157); Toulouse-Lautrec Museum, Albi, France (page 161); United Press International, New York (page 47).

Quotation on page 20 from *Edith Wharton: A Biography* by R.W.B. Lewis, © 1975 by Harper & Row Publishers, Inc.; quotation on page 263 from *Bloomsbury: A House of Lions* by Leon Edel, © 1979 by J. B. Lippincott & Company, reprinted by permission of Harper & Row Publishers, Inc.

Inquiries should be addressed to Crown Publishers, Inc., One Park Avenue, New York, New York 10016

Printed in the United States of America

Published simultaneously in Canada by General Publishing Company Limited

Library of Congress Cataloging in Publication Data

Birnkrant, Ruth.
    Fascinating facts about love, sex & marriage

    1. Sex—Miscellanea. 2. Love—Miscellanea.
I. Title.
HQ12.B55 1981   306.7   81-812
                              AACR2

ISBN: 0-517-545055

10 9 8 7 6 5 4 3 2 1

First Edition

Contents

Aubrey Beardsley's version of *Messalina Returning from the Bath*—the site of many of the empress' sexual adventures.

Actors
(Also see Hollywood)

The beauty and talent of Rome's leading actor, Mnester, evoked the passions of Caligula, among many others, but it was the empress Messalina who was responsible for his execution.

She stopped a play in the middle of the performance and commanded him to follow her home—and to bed. (Anyone who disobeyed her imperious sexual commands was subject to the death penalty.)

She kept Mnester away from the theater, set him up as her lover and had statues of him made and cast in gold. When her husband, Claudius, finally condemned her to death, Mnester and many of her other lovers were also executed.

Mlle. Georges, reigning queen of the Comédie-Française, was Napoleon's favorite. But when he divorced Josephine and married Marie Louise, determined to have a son at last, he put Mlle. Georges aside to devote his waning energies to that imperial necessity.

She grew old and fat, her last stage appearance being one of great pathos. The part required that she sink to her knees, pray and stand again. But struggle as she would, her age and her obesity made it impossible for her to regain her feet. She was unable to restrain her tears of despair, and it seemed to some a perfect metaphor for the tragedy of a former reigning favorite of both the theater and the emperor.

Adah Menken was an American actress who was also a poet. Stunningly beautiful, she had had four—some say five—marriages and many affairs. Among others whom she knew were Walt Whitman, Mark Twain, Bret Harte, Henry Wadsworth Longfellow (who was at her bedside when she died), Alexandre Dumas and Charles Dickens.

Her first marriage was to a frail Jewish violinist. When he died she married his exact opposite, John C. Heenan, the powerful heavyweight boxing champion of the world.

1

She solicited advice about her poetry from Algernon Swinburne, a poet of extraordinary talent, who was also a homosexual. He was struck by her beauty, if not by her talent, and made feeble—some say heroic—efforts to become her lover.

Friends of his urged Adah Menken to be kind to him, and she agreed to do so. But her efforts proved fruitless. She reported to his friends that the utmost Swinburne could manage was to bite her shoulder.

Born to a fishmonger, inmate of a bawdy house at fifteen, actress at sixteen, Nell Gwyn became the mistress of King Charles II at seventeen. Or rather co-mistress, her rival being the Duchess of Portsmouth, who was a Catholic.

One day when a crowd pelted the closed coach Nell was riding in, thinking it was the duchess's, whom they hated, Nell stuck her head out and shouted, "Stop! I am the Protestant whore!"

On his deathbed Charles told his brother James, "Let not poor Nelly starve."

Sir Peter Lely, *Nell Gwyn.*

Sarah Bernhardt posing in the famous casket in which she was rumored to have had love trysts. She bought it when she was twenty-one. Sixty years later she was finally buried in it.

Sarah (the divine Sarah) Bernhardt, the reigning queen of the stage for half a century, numbered among her lovers some of the kings of Europe, as well as a notable assortment of princes, dukes, archdukes and others.

Divine or not, rather early in her career, Bernhardt experienced certain intimations of mortality, causing her to order a coffin for herself. It was a sumptuous affair, in keeping with her extravagant style of life, and she took to carrying it with her during some of her tours.

Given her bravura persona, it was inevitable that the gossip vendors of the time would make lurid capital of this bizarre act, declaring that Sarah used the coffin as a "love nest." Between the time when she acquired it and sixty years later when she was buried in it, dozens of men had been named as having shared its accommodations with her.

Cornelia Otis Skinner who wrote a Bernhardt biography dismissed these gamey reports as baseless gossip.

"I've had twenty years of perfect companionship with a man among men," Katharine Hepburn said after Spencer Tracy's death—the only statement she ever made about their romance.

Katharine Hepburn and Spencer Tracy—along with Sidney Poitier—being directed in *Guess Who's Coming to Dinner?*

The last picture in which they played together (there were nineteen in all) was *Guess Who's Coming to Dinner?* He was a dying man. He knew it, she knew it and Lloyd's of London knew it—and therefore would not insure his life, even for just the duration of the film's shooting schedule.

Hepburn begged him not to take the role, but he insisted.

Each scene was a drama in itself. Would he survive the scene? Or even the shot? By sheer will, and with Hepburn nursing him through the schedule, he managed it. When the director triumphantly shouted, "Cut! Print it!" in the last shot of the film, Tracy exulted, "I made it! I made it!"

There were tears in everyone's eyes on the set, even the most case-hardened.

There is one line in that film which in itself may well have been the reason Tracy undertook the part: He is supposed to be withholding his blessing to his daughter's marriage to Sidney Poitier. Finally, he yields, saying to Hepburn, "If what they feel for each other is even half of what we felt, then that is everything."

With this line, perhaps, Tracy, the most private of men, could tell the world that he and his Kate had shared a life that made his approaching death easier to take.

In 1955, at the age of twenty-four, Jimmy Dean *(East of Eden, Rebel Without a Cause)* died in an automobile crash. But he continued to receive mail from his devoted followers at the rate of five thousand letters a week. They could not—and many still do not—accept the idea that he was mortal.

Mary Miles Mintner, a beautiful young motion-picture star, leaned down, kissed William Desmond Taylor full on the lips, straightened up and declared that she distinctly heard him whisper, "I shall always love you, Mary."

There would have been nothing very singular about this except that at the moment the famous director was lying quite dead in a funeral casket, and the lady who heard his love avowal was among those suspected of murdering him. And not only Mary, but her mother as well. The very popular Mabel Norman was also under serious investigation by the district attorney.

There were other suspects too, for Taylor was a man who could manipulate several mistresses simultaneously. At least until one of them decided otherwise.

The state was unable to prove a case against anyone, but as a result of the lurid revelations, the film careers of Mintner and Norman came to an untimely end.

The "marrying Mdivanis" were two brothers, "princes," in exile from Soviet Georgia. When one married Pola Negri and the other Mae Murray, some questions were raised about the soundness of their titles, but none at all about their financial judgment, for both women were highly successful Hollywood stars.

As soon as they exhausted the fortunes they adored, the brothers went on to greener pastures. When Mae Murray came on hard times— very hard times indeed, for she was arrested as a vagrant—her princely former husband, though well married again, refused to help her.

It is felt by many that Montgomery Clift's death and the terrible years of agony that preceded it were due in significant measure to his feeling that he must at all costs conceal his homosexuality.

Gloria Swanson also rejoiced—temporarily—in a title, as the Marquise de la Falaise de la Coudray. Happily, she recovered and detached herself in a timely way. (Aided, according to her published memoir, by Joseph P. Kennedy, father of John F. Kennedy, whose ardor she was unable to resist.)

During the period when Tallulah Bankhead was carrying on an active bisexual life, she met Joan Crawford, who had just married Douglas Fairbanks, Jr. After congratulating Crawford, she said, "I've had an affair with Douglas—my next will be with you."

(This was during the Great Depression when, with hundreds of banks failing, it was said that "Tallulah was the only solvent Bankhead in the country!")

Some of the greatest love affairs I've ever known have involved one actor—unassisted.   —WILSON MIZNER

When Ingrid Bergman was at the very height of her illustrious career, she fell in love with Roberto Rossellini, the Italian director, and had a child by him. Hedda Hopper and Louella Parsons, the syndicated gossip columnists, professing outrage at Bergman's fall from grace, succeeded in frightening the film studios into blacklisting her.

On March 14, 1950, Senator Edwin C. Johnson felt the situation grave enough to make a thunderous attack in the U.S. Senate against Bergman for her "assault upon the institution of marriage," explaining that she was "a powerful influence for evil . . ." and therefore must not be permitted to return to the United States.

Years later, after Vanessa Redgrave and several other stars refused to enter matrimonial relations just to "legitimize" their children, Bergman was finally allowed by the nervous film industry to resume her career.

W. C. Fields, a true comic genius but a victim of paranoia, was known for his lifelong misanthropism. (He once said of someone, "He can't be all bad—hates children and dogs.")

As he lay dying, he said to his last companion: "Goddamn the whole frigging world and everyone in it, except you, Carlotta."

There were several attempts at suicide among the 100,000 grief-stricken fans at the funeral of Rudolph Valentino, the first of the great screen lovers.

The death of Rudolph Valentino, one of the greatest of all screen lovers *(The Sheik,* etc.), was the subject of conflicting rumors of suicide and murder, despite the medical report of peritonitis resulting from an appendectomy.

Many rumors were circulated impugning his masculinity, especially after his divorce from the exotic Natacha Rambova who declared that their marriage had never been consummated. But the legions of his worshipful fans were never in doubt that he was the world's greatest lover. More than one hundred thousand of them turned out for his funeral, among whom there were several attempts of suicide.

It has been pointed out that marriages among theater people tend to be more lasting than those among film actors. Witness: Alfred Lunt and Lynn Fontanne, Hume Cronyn and Jessica Tandy, Anne Jackson and Eli Wallach, Ruth Gordon and Garson Kanin, Helen Hayes and Charles MacArthur, Jack Gilford and Madeline Lee, Charles Laughton and Elsa Lanchester, Danny Kaye and Sylvia Fine, George Burns and Gracie Allen, Jack Benny and Mary Livingston, Zero Mostel and Kathryn Harkins.

Al Jolson was fond of telling the story of his marriage night, when his bride's dog, believing his mistress was being attacked, jumped on the bed and bit hard into Jolson's big toe, holding on long enough to dampen Jolson's ardor—at least for that night.

The story is a precise parallel to Napoleon's experience with Josephine's dog, except that it was the great general's calf that was bitten. The effect, however, was identical.

Shelley Winters writes that Marilyn Monroe said to her, "Wouldn't it be nice to sleep with the most attractive men and not get emotionally involved?"

They drew up lists of candidates for such ad hoc affairs, Monroe's ending with Albert Einstein.

WINTERS: "There's no way you can sleep with Einstein. He's the most famous scientist of the century, and besides, he's an old man."

MONROE: "I hear he's very healthy."

"I don't know how many of her choices she achieved," Winters writes, "but after her death I saw a large framed photograph of Albert Einstein [on the piano]. On it was written, 'To Marilyn, with respect and thanks. Albert Einstein.'"

The list of notables who later shared her bed was far more varied and extensive than she envisioned at that time. She was married to one of baseball's "immortals" and to one of America's most leading playwrights; she had "affairs" with a U.S. president and his brother; with one of the most popular and enduring singing stars of all time; with the most celebrated macho film stars; with the heads of great corporations.

But she died alone in her bed from an overdose of barbiturates, really from a lack of genuine love and from a disastrous loss of self-esteem.

Alfred Lunt and Lynn Fontanne, one of the greatest theatrical teams of the American theater, were married to each other and lived together happily until the day he died, though he was gay.

Similarly, though Charles Laughton was a homosexual, he lived with his actress wife, Elsa Lanchester, for thirty-three years until his death.

Adultery
(Also see Bastards; Law; Jealousy)

Though Julia, the emperor Augustus's only child, was well known to have legions of lovers, her five children all resembled her husband.

Her explanation: "I take on passengers only when the boat is full."

Like Empress Messalina, she would venture out at night to the Forum, near the statue of Marsyas, where the prostitutes would gather, and do business with passersby.

In ancient Egypt, if a wife was unfaithful she and her lover were bound together and thrown into the river to drown. In later times, the lover could be castrated and the wife's nose severed.

(In 1977, in Saudi Arabia, a nineteen-year-old princess was publicly executed for a sexual affair with a student. The boy was beheaded.)

Guillaume de Cabestan, a troubadour, was killed by Sir Raimon de Rossilho for making love to his wife. That night Sir Raimon fed his wife the cooked heart of her lover. When she learned the nature of the dish she'd eaten, she committed suicide.

In 1660, Edmond Andros, as governor of the Dominion of New England, was accused of "admitting the squaws dayly to him, or else he went out and lodged with them."

"I allow you every latitude," the courtiers would lecture their wives at Versailles, "except footmen and Princes of the Blood."

Charlemagne's daughter and her married lover had to cross a muddy field to reach the castle. In order to avoid leaving his telltale footprints in the mud, she carried him on her back for almost a quarter of a mile.

Héloise and Abélard, from a manuscript of 1532. Their illicit love survived the ferocious penalty imposed upon Abélard.

The highly gifted theologian/philosopher, Abélard, having contracted an unlawful passion for his young, beautiful and intellectual student, Héloise, was castrated by her uncle. She spent the rest of her life in a convent, loving him as he loved her, to the very end. This was of the stuff that appealed to the romantically inclined and has thus been celebrated for eight hundred years.

Catherine Howard on the scaffold: "I have not wronged the king [Henry VIII]. But it is true that long before the king took me, I loved Culpepper, and I wish to God I had done as he wished me, for at the time the king wanted to take me, he urged me to say I was pledged to him. If I had done as he advised me, I should not die this death, nor would he. I would rather have had him for a husband than be mistress of the world, but sin blinded me, and the greed of grandeur; and since mine is the fault, mine also is the suffering, and my great sorrow is that Culpepper should have had to die through me."

She turned to the headsman. "Pray, hasten with thy office. . . . I die a queen, but I would rather die the wife of Culpepper. God have mercy on my soul. Good people, I beg you pray for me."

(Queen Catherine's declaration calls to mind Heloise's: "How often I have protested that it was infinitely preferable to me to live with Abelard as his mistress than with any other as empress of the world.")

Under Calvin's rule in Geneva, fornication was a cause for exile and adultery was a cause for death. (Even singing, dancing, cursing or eating too many courses in one meal were crimes.)

If young people were seen to be conversing too familiarly they were suspected of "fornication" and punished.

Saint Anselm, Archbishop of Canterbury, wrote to the king of Ireland (about 1100), "We hear that in your kingdom men exchange their wives for those of other men as freely and as publicly as anyone changes one horse for another." Some scholars disagree with the archbishop's findings.

The House of Lords tried George IV's wife, Queen Caroline, charging her with an adulterous affair while in Italy. She was acquitted, despite the efforts of the Duke of Wellington, then prime minister.

The idea that an English queen could sin with an Italian shocked and delighted the nation.

During the War of Independence, the British general Sir Henry Clinton took as his mistress the wife of one of his officers—but only after it became clear to him that the officer wished his wife "to enjoy a certain degree of intimacy" with his commanding general. The husband was then advanced in rank. General Richard Howe objected to this arrangement, though he himself was rewarding an officer who was complaisant about *his* wife's relationship with the general.

Mary Dyer, a Quaker who was hanged in Boston as an irreconcilable heretic, was rumored to have given birth to a monster as a result of her unnatural liaison with some netherworld creature. William Bradford, the leader of the Pilgrims, was curious about the exact "forme of that monster."

The Dutch were as interested as the English in "wondrously horrible births." A monument was erected in the fifteenth century in Leiden to the memory of the Countess of Holland for having "365 children in one birth."

The Chevalier de La Tour Landry related the incident of the couple who, in medieval times, defiled a church by having sex at the altar.

They were caught and tied "like a dog and a bitch together." He warned females not to be alone with a man, even a priest—except at confession.

One American court decided that a woman who opted for artificial insemination without her husband's consent was guilty of adultery.

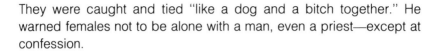

Advisers
(Also see Charms, Folklore and Magic

Kamasutra, possibly the first "how-to" book on sexual love, describes ten different ways to kiss and sixty-four methods of foreplay, as well as variations in the sexual act itself. It also gives recipes for potency.

This book was outlawed in the United States.

But *The Joy of Sex* has sold over 1.5 million copies in hard cover and over 4 million copies in oversized paperback.

In old Rome, no marriage would be solemnized unless the family augur first examined the entrails of a sacrificed animal and declared that the signs were favorable.

Suetonius says that when Julius Caesar dreamed that he raped his mother, his official dream interpreter told him that it meant that he would conquer the earth.

(A modern commentator remarked that these days if a man dreams that he conquered the earth he would be advised by his analyst that he really desired his mother.)

Benjamin Franklin advised a young man to choose an older woman as a lover for eight reasons, among which are they are more discreet; "the sin is less" because "the debauching of a Virgin may be her ruin"; the pleasure with an old woman is at least equal and frequently superior; that "there is no hazard of children"; and lastly, "they are so grateful!"

Franklin doesn't appear to have followed his own advice, at least in an affair in which there was more than a "hazard" of a child: There was William, illegitimate, who was on the British side during the Revolution.

___

During the innocent 1920s, Elinor Glyn, author of the "sensational" novel *Three Weeks,* was generous in her advice to young women. A sample:

"Never give easily. Do not give at all until you know the man is really attracted to you, and even then only in small doses. For man is an instinctive hunter and he is by nature polygamous.

"It is unnatural for him to be faithful to you."

___

Not too long ago Beatrice Fairfax and Dorothy Dix, in their newspaper columns, were advising thousands of "Blue Eyes," and "Perplexeds" that they ought never to kiss a boy the first few times they dated (and if possible not at all until they were "engaged"), to remain chaste no matter how close the wedding date was, and even not to jump over puddles of water because boys might see the reflection of their legs— even thighs!—in the water.

The changing nature of the times is nowhere more manifest than in the context of the problems presented to the syndicated successors of Beatrice Fairfax. The following items are from the columns of a single newspaper during a period of only five weeks:

1. A fifteen-year-old girl with a baby fathered by a sixteen-year-old boy. She wants to keep it, her parents are opposed. What should she do?

2. A woman with five children who feels "gypped." She was one of ten children and always had to take care of her brothers and sisters. And now, at thirty-two, with five children of her own, she has never "had a chance to be me, to be young. I don't know how to get rid of the hate I feel for my husband and for all men who make women have babies they don't want."

3. A case of incest.

4. A distraught woman who has just found out that her parents have never married and that she is therefore illegitimate. Does that make "my own babies bastards"?

5. Should a woman tell her husband about her affair with their neighbor?

6. Should she marry a very rich man simply to enable her children to go to college?

7. A woman worried that since the death of her father her mother seems to be turning lesbian.

8. A woman of twenty-six with five children who wants her husband to have a vasectomy.

Among lighter items:

9. A twenty-nine-year-old bachelor who prefers only very, very fat women to have sex with. His best experience was with a woman who weighed four hundred pounds.

10. A justice of the peace, incensed when he found out that the "bride" of the couple he had married was really a man.

11. To Dear Abby, a twelve-year-old, signing her name Never Been Kissed, asking for advice about how to kiss a boy. "Should the girl quit breathing? Am I supposed to move my head? Or do I just move my lips? One last thing—what am I supposed to do with my nose?"

12. "Dear Meg: I work with a circus. My problem is Renata, my partner on the high wire. I've been in love with her for two years and I thought it was mutual until last April when I dropped her in practice. She hasn't spoken to me since."

13. "Paul and I are both normal in every sense of the word. It all started this way: I am five feet eleven, and Paul is five feet five. We are as compatible as two people can be, but we have always felt somewhat conspicuous in public. For that reason, I stopped wearing heels.

"One day I bought some women's wedgie shoes in Paul's size and gave them to him. He tried them on, found them to be very comfortable and was delighted with the extra height they provided. After wearing these wedgies a few times, he wanted another pair. Now he refuses anything else. Just for fun, I put some makeup on him and got him a woman's wig, and we went to dinner that way. We loved it! Then I started to dress like a man, and now we do it all the time. I assure you we are sexually normal. My husband dresses as a man for work. We switch roles for fun only when we go out."

Animals

Janet and the man who dearly loved her died within a short time of each other, possibly at the very same time.

He was an English professor from Philadelphia, while she lived in a cage in New York City's Central Park Zoo, the oldest lioness in captivity.

Every weekend, year after year, he would journey to New York to visit with Janet and to murmur to her, "Ah, there, my beauty, my Janet," as they gazed into each other's eyes, disregarding the startled looks of the other visitors.

One day, a keeper at the Zoo, Mr. Clement, noticed that the professor seemed to be ailing. He didn't come the following week, nor the next, nor ever again.

Until she died several weeks later, Janet kept her eyes fixed on the door through which the professor always entered.

Later, Mr. Clement received word that the professor did indeed die at almost the same time as "the great and beloved lioness"—to use his words.

An ornithologist remarked that the male of the human species, tending less and less to exert himself in the courting process, should take lessons from the gray heron and other birds.

The male gray heron goes through all sorts of acrobatics to prove its credentials to the female, even looping the loop.

The lapwing will fly close to the ground, emitting a mating call followed by a vocal change or a steep vertical flight. Then with a wild, exultant cry, it swoops down, turning somersaults and even flying on its back. On the ground again he does little tripping runs and then bows a number of times to the female, who makes encouraging sounds as he performs for her.

The male crestless gardener bowerbird of New Guinea decorates with orchids the hutlike bower it builds for its courtship display. It periodically replaces the wilted blossoms with fresh ones to attract the female.

In the incubation process, the male pigeon broods from 10 A.M. to 2:30 P.M., the female taking over for the rest of the day.

The male black swan is even more responsive, brooding from 10 A.M. to 5 P.M. And the African male ostrich sits from 5 P.M. through the night until 8 A.M. (The cock ostrich being jet black is less conspicuous to predators than the female.)

The females among the songster birds brood mostly alone, as do owls and birds of prey.

Even after months at sea, away from one another, male and female penguins who have previously mated recognize one another when they return to their nesting places. And when they do, they dance together in an ecstatic display, voice their pleasure and presently go about the business of reproducing themselves.

By the time the female lays her egg she has not eaten for three weeks. The male takes over the incubation while the female goes to sea to feed and recuperate.

During this time (at least two weeks) the male will do his stint despite cold and wind and snowstorms, until the female returns. Later, after the egg is hatched, both parents will feed and defend the chick against predators.

The penguins will lose up to seventy-five pounds during the incubation period.

Darwin relates: Animal courtship is carried on by single pairs or at special nuptial mass meetings resembling those held by some primitive tribes whose unmarried young people gather on certain days of the year to select partners. Of the common magpie, Darwin reports: "They had the habit of assembling very early in the spring at particular spots where they would be seen in flocks, chattering, sometimes fighting, bustling and flying about the trees. Shortly after the meeting they all separated and were observed paired for the season. This was known as the 'great magpie marriage.'"

In some species of fish the male will fertilize the eggs in its mouth and thereby deprive itself of food for many days.

The male ocelot is possibly the only one in the cat family who shares with the female the job of bringing up the young.

Even bacteria, which until recently were thought to be sexless, have male and female parts.

Among whiptail lizards of the genus *Cnemidophorus* (a slender reptile in the southwest desert), there are no males. The females give birth to females, who give birth to females, ad infinitum.

Baboons will defend to the death their families—which evoked from a domestic relations judge the comment that deserting fathers who used baboon as a derogatory term should be forced to live among them and apologize to them three times a day for at least thirty days.

The devotion among a family of baboons exceeds that of many humans.

When the queen bee takes off on her nuptial flight she is followed by a swarm of drones all eager to be the lucky one who impregnates her. The race is to the swift, but for his pains the queen often will deprive him of his testes. Unable to survive this indignity, the drone dies, unaware that he has accomplished the single act for which nature had equipped him.

If he somehow survives the nuptial flight, he is shut out of the hive and soon dies.

There are some female spiders who, larger and more powerful than the male, will very likely eat him after he has mated with her. The canny male will often watch her covertly until she has satisfied her hunger on foreign insects before he courts her. (Sometimes he strums on the web as though on a guitar and observes whether she is responding to the vibes he creates.)

Sometimes a cagey male spider will protect himself by catching her asleep and immobilizing her, tying her up before he mounts her.

The curator of mammals in the Hermann Park Zoo in Houston tried an experiment on a male and female gorilla "couple" who failed to couple. He brought in a television set and turned it on to different programs, including those showing various stages of love relationships.

The gorilla couple were interested enough to watch for hours on end, but it did nothing for *their* love life. (Causing one wife, who calls herself a "TV widow" to say: "I could have told them not to waste their time.")

"We're probably going to go to artificial insemination," the curator said philosophically.

Rape is unknown among animals (except for the human species), the willingness of the female being a necessary element in the mating process.

Artists

Leonardo da Vinci was arrested and accused of a homosexual act.

His desperate need for affection attached itself to a beautiful boy, Giacomo de Caprotti, who for twenty-six years stole from him and otherwise shamefully exploited da Vinci's feeling for him.

Because of his affection for him, Michelangelo endured Tommaso Cavalieri's often savage treatment of him for thirty-two years. But Cavalieri was present at his bedside when he died.

After his wife, Saskia, died, Rembrandt (Rembrandt van Rijn) lived with Hendrickje Stoffels, the woman who had been their servant. They did not marry because the small inheritance from Saskia's estate would have been terminated.

They lived contentedly with each other until she died.

Camille Pissarro, too, lived with the domestic who had served his family, and they also did not marry because Pissarro's support would have been cut off. After many years and several children, his mother finally relented and they were married, to everyone's joy.

Their life was a good one.

Camille Pissarro, *Self-portrait*.

19

Vincent van Gogh, *Self-portrait.* He sheltered a pregnant prostitute and offered to marry her.

That in his madness Vincent van Gogh cut off his ear and offered it as a gift to a prostitute is very well known; but there was an earlier incident that prefigured this self-mutilation:

When a girl he loved fled to her family in Amsterdam, van Gogh followed her and pleaded to be allowed to see her. When her family refused, he put his hand in the flame of a lamp, saying, "Let me see her for only as long as I can keep my hand in the flame."

As his hand burned they were horrified. They shut the lamp off and ordered him out of the house.

He never saw the girl again.

Soon thereafter he gave refuge to a sick and pregnant street-walker and offered to marry her, though he himself lacked clothing and food, for there were no buyers for his works. (In May 1980 one of his paintings sold for more than $5 million.)

Edouard Manet fathered a child and tried to pass it off as his mistress's brother.

Fra Filippo Lippi was chaplain to the nuns of Santee Margherita at Prato. He eloped with a young nun who was pregnant by him.

The baby became Filippino Lippi, also a fine painter.

Pope Pius, on the plea of the Medicis, released Filippo and the nun from their vows so that they could marry.

In 1870, Paul Cézanne had a child with a model, Hortense Fiquet, whom he finally married in 1884—when he no longer loved her.

Maurice Utrillo was illegitimate. Son of a writer who would not marry his mother (who had talent as a painter and acrobat and had posed for Renoir), Utrillo early took to drink and was finally put away as a madman.

When Amedeo Modigliani died, Jeanne Hébuterne, his wife, threw herself across his body, covered it with kisses, then went to her father's house and killed herself by jumping from the roof.

Amedeo Modigliani's portrait of his wife, Jeanne Hébuterne.

Not only did the friends of Jean Auguste Dominique Ingres think that at thirty-three he should have a wife, but they selected her for him: Madeline Chapelle, whom he married immediately, and lived happily with for forty-five years.

When she died he was unable to work for three years. Then, at the age of seventy-two, he met and married a forty-year-old woman and immediately became productive again. He was seventy-eight when he painted the famous *La Source.*

Authors
(Also see Poets)

The wife of an apothecary explained to her friend a sexual episode with D. H. Lawrence: "I had to. He was over at our house struggling with a poem he couldn't finish. So I took him upstairs and gave him sex. He came downstairs and finished the poem."

Honoré de Balzac generally stopped short of a climax in his lovemaking because he believed that semen was the brain's most distinguished product and that his own supply was accountable for his success as an author. As he joined his friends at dinner one evening, he announced tragically, "Today I lost a book."

William Congreve, the dramatist, had as his lover the Duchess of Marlborough. Deranged by his death, she ordered a life-sized dummy made up and attached a replica of Congreve's face to it. She spoke to it as though it were alive, undressed it every night and bedded it down beside her, and in the morning dressed it carefully and lovingly.

From time to time she called the doctor in because Congreve "had become ill." The doctor would go through the charade of examination, diagnosis and prescription.

The elder Alexandre Dumas, on the difference between his son and himself:

"If you locked me in my bedroom with five women, pens, paper, ink and a play to be written, by the end of an hour I'd have written the play and had the five women."

Prodigious in sexual affairs as in his literary output, Dumas was guilty of only one marriage—a very temporary one, to be sure. One night he caught his wife in bed with a lover, took pity on the frightened man and suggested that since the night was frigid, the three of them should share the one bed in the house. Even with the additional heat generated by Dumas's large body, the lover shivered violently through the balance of the night. In the morning Dumas gracefully sent the man on his way, and soon used the occasion to regain his legal freedom.

When Charles Dickens's daughter, Kate, died at the age of eighty-nine, she left the following statement about him:

"I loved my father better than any man in the world. I loved him for his faults. My father was a wicked man—a very wicked man."

Charles Dickens and daughters Kate and Mamie.

Prosper Mérimée and George Sand had a single disastrous night together. She wrote her friend Marie Dorval: "I slept with Mérimée last night. He is less than nothing."

She didn't reveal—but he did—that when he departed next morning he contemptuously left a five-franc piece on her dresser.

Love is a bottomless pit. It is a cormorant—a harpy that devours everything.   —JONATHAN SWIFT

Marie Henri Beyle (as Stendhal, he wrote *The Red and the Black, Charterhouse of Parma,* among others), writing about his mother, who died when he was seven:

"I wanted to cover my mother with kisses, and for her to have no clothes on. I abhorred my father when he came in and interrupted my kisses."

All his life he ruthlessly analyzed himself: his passions, his motives, his strength and weaknesses, and in that respect anticipated Freudian techniques.

In planning his "campaigns" to win the affections of a woman, he advised himself:

Attack!

Attack!

Attack!

In a four-hundred-page essay on love, Stendhal invented the theory of "crystallization," the process by which the imagination of the lover attaches all sorts of illusions of perfection to the beloved, while his own self-interest becomes purified, and his ego itself becomes "incurably" identified with the person loved.

Jean Jacques Rousseau's father never tired of reminding him that he was the cause of his mother's death. (She died a few days after giving birth to him.) "Let us talk of your beautiful mama," his father would say. And the boy would respond, "Very well, Father, and then we will cry." And cry they would.

In his *Confessions,* Rousseau revealed that he felt what he called incestuous urges toward the woman who gave him shelter and whom he called "Mama."

Paul Gavarni's print of George Sand and escort. Whatever she wore, said or wrote and whomever she loved, she created scandal.

The Goncourt brothers (in their jointly written journal) shared identical views on art, literature, politics and their attraction/revulsion for women.

The de Goncourt brothers, in their joint journal: "One week of love disgusts us for three months"; "Woman is an evil, stupid animal"; "Woman: the most beautiful and most admirable of laying machines."

To a friend who wept because of being betrayed by a woman, Edmund de Goncourt said, "Dammit all, Charles, forget about that bitch and let's go to a brothel."

Charles, with great tears trickling down his cheeks sobbed, "I've bought her twelve hundred francs' worth of jewels."

"One day you'll have an income of eighty thousand francs a year. Why, with all that, I'd walk on a woman as if she was a pavement," Goncourt replied.

Voltaire's mistress was the Marquise du Châtelet. They were lovers for sixteen years—with the consent of the marquis.

Change everything but your loves, he counseled.

Vassily Rosanov, a young writer, fell in love and married the tempestuous Appolinariya Prokofievna Suslova, twenty years older, simply because Dostoevsky had once been her lover.

Rosanov deified Dostoevsky, proclaimed himself a disciple, and by possessing the same woman raised his sexual relations with her to a religious sacrament, a holy ecstasy.

Feodor Dostoevsky *(Brothers Karamazov, Crime and Punishment)* faced an execution squad, spent eight years in Siberia and a tortured life thereafter, but he never lost his powerful sexual drive.

Even on the eve of her wedding, the mother of Edith Wharton *(In Old New York)* refused to enlighten her about the mysteries of the marriage bed.

Edith Wharton, one of America's outstanding writers, *(Age of Innocence, Ethan Frome)* came of a rich and influential family but at age twenty-four, and about to be married, she was ignorant of sex. R.W.B. Lewis in his biography of Edith Wharton writes: "A few days before the wedding, Edith plucked up her courage and went to her mother, her heart beating wildly, to ask 'what marriage was really like.' Lucretia's [her mother's] face took on the look of icy disapproval which Edith most feared, and she answered with impatience: 'I never heard such a ridiculous question!'

"Edith's tormented anxiety spurred her to continue: 'I'm afraid, Mamma—I want to know what will happen to me.' After an awful silence, during which Lucretia's expression changed to disgust, she said with a distinct effort: 'You've seen enough pictures and statues in your life. Haven't you noticed that men are . . . made differently from women?' Edith faltered out an uncomprehending 'Yes.' 'Well, then?' Edith stood staring blankly at her mother, quite unable to grasp her meaning, until Lucretia brought the conversation to an abrupt end: 'Then for heaven's sake don't ask me any more silly questions. You can't be as stupid as you pretend.'"

You have only to look these "happy couples" in the face to see they have never been in love, or in hate, or any other high passion, all their days. When you see a dish of fruit, at dessert, you sometimes set your affections upon one particular peach or nectarine, watch it with some anxiety as it comes around the table and feel quite a sensible disappointment when it is taken by someone else. . . . Well, I should say this was about as high a passion as generally leads to marriage.

You wonder if it was always equally dull and spiritless, and possession equally cold.   —ROBERT LOUIS STEVENSON

Leo Tolstoy's terrible scene with his wife four months before he died (1910):

She had found his secret diaries and in her desperation she read aloud to him an item he had written sixty years before:

"I have never been in love with women. . . . I have fallen in love with men very often."

In his posthumously published novelette, *The Devil,* Tolstoy couldn't decide whether to end it with the murder of the peasant woman by the passionately obsessed hero, or by his suicide.

The reason for this was that the peasant character referred to was based upon a real woman, about whom Tolstoy had unresolved guilt feelings.

To say that you can love one person all your life is just like saying that one candle will continue burning as long as you live.

—LEO TOLSTOY, *The Kreutzer Sonata*

Such masters of the English language as Swift, Carlyle and Dickens addressed their loved ones, respectively, as "Dood mollow," "My little Screamikin," "dearest titmouse." And to George Bernard Shaw, Mrs. Patrick Campbell was his "loveliest, dovelliest."

James Thurber claimed that generally a writer "would rather leap into print with his lady than leap into bed with her."

On the other hand, John Keats: "I have met women who I really think would like to be married to a poem and given away by a novel."

BOSWELL: "Pray, sir, do you not suppose that there are fifty women in the world with whom a man may be as happy as with one woman in particular?"

JOHNSON: "Ay, sir, fifty thousand."

BOSWELL: "Then, sir, you are not of the opinion with some who imagine that certain men and certain women are made for each other and that they cannot be happy if they miss their counterparts."

JOHNSON: "To be sure not, sir. I believe marriage would in general be as happy and often more so if they were all made by the lord chancellor—without the parties having any choice in the matter."

—JAMES BOSWELL, *The Life of Samuel Johnson*

For a man to pretend to understand a woman is bad manners, for him to really understand her is bad morals.   —HENRY JAMES

When I was a young man I had a mistress, a miller's daughter, whom I used to see when I went out hunting. She would never accept anything from me. One day, however, she said to me, "You must bring me a present." "What do you want?" "Bring me a bar of soap." When I did so, she disappeared, came back covered with blushes, held out her scented hands and said, "Now kiss my hands as you kiss the hands of the ladies in the drawing rooms of St. Petersburg."

I threw myself on my knees before her.   —IVAN TURGENEV

George Bernard Shaw to Ellen Terry: "Up to the time I was twenty-nine, I was too shabby for any woman to tolerate me. I stalked about in a decaying green coat, cuffs trimmed with the scissors, terrible boots, and so on. Then I got a job to do and bought a suit of clothes with the proceeds. A lady immediately invited me to tea, threw her arms round me, and said she adored me. I permitted her to adore, being intensely curious on the subject. Never having regarded myself as an attractive man, I was surprised; but I kept up appearances successfully. Since that time, whenever I have been left alone in a room with a female, she has invariably thrown her arms round me and declared she adored me. It is fate. Therefore beware. If you allow yourself to be left alone with me for a single moment, you will certainly throw your arms round me and declare you adore me."

The fickleness of the women I love is only equaled by the infernal constancy of the women who love me.   —GEORGE BERNARD SHAW

Anthony Comstock, head of the Society for the Suppression of Vice, said, "George Bernard Shaw is an Irish smut dealer."

The great satirist Jonathan Swift *(Gulliver's Travels)* lived out a tortured, repressed sexual/emotional existence, and in turn tortured the lives of the two women whom he loved and who loved him. He paid assiduous court to "Stella" and "Vanessa," but withheld himself physically from them.

After years of suffering, he finally yielded to Stella's pleas and married her secretly, but even then refused to live with her or have sexual relations with her. He went so far as to require that she invite other guests to be present when he visited her.

He died insane.

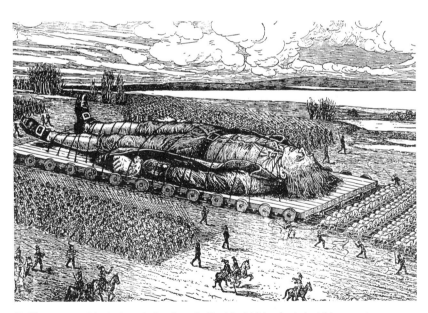

Gulliver was able to break the bonds that held him fast, but his creator, Jonathan Swift, remained a lifelong slave to his phobias about sex.

In a sensational divorce trial a film star's diary was used against her. Among the items was one describing a night with George Kaufman, the playwright. "Twenty times, dear diary. Twenty times! . . . I don't know how he does it!"

Because she had affairs with such idols as John Barrymore, and had reported no such heroic performances from them, some writers suggested that even the most slouching, hollow-chested and heavily bespectacled pen pushers were more than a match for the most celebrated of thespians.

Autoeroticism

Samuel Terry was accused in Boston of "chafing his yard" as he faced the outside wall of the church during sermon time. We know the penalty—six lashes—but not what the sermon was about.

According to ancient Hebraic law, a man was required to marry his brother's widow when she was childless. Any child of this marriage was then considered to be the first brother's, with rights of inheritance, etc. (known as the law of the levirate).

When his brother died, Onan did indeed marry Tamar, the widow, but he "spilled his seed upon the ground" (whether by masturbation or by withdrawal is still debated). For this dereliction Onan was struck dead by God.

Unable to achieve motherhood by the sons, Tamar tricked their father into fatherhood (by posing as a prostitute).

Though masturbation has been considered a most grievous sin, there is nothing in either the Old or the New Testament to support this dogma. Nor is there any evidence that more ancient societies prohibited the practice.

Until lately it was believed that, among other evils, masturbation led to loss of virility, of hair, of sight and of sanity itself. (Some still believe it.)

Various measures were used to prevent boys (we seldom hear about girls in this connection) from "sinning": cold showers, the wearing of heavy mittens at night—as well as keeping one's hands outside of the blanket, no matter how cold the temperature—and never, never keeping one's hands in one's pockets. Prayers were considered helpful.

In cases of the most egregious offenders, machines were constructed for nighttime duty. One of the more extreme examples: Both of the boy's hands would be tied to the bedposts, giving him a crucified appearance. In addition, an iron cage was fitted over the boy's genitals and locked. Sad to say that even these sensible measures were sometimes of no avail when "she-devils" invaded the boy's dreams.

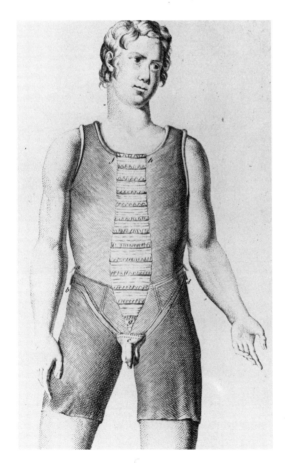

One of the many devices designed to protect boys from "self-abuse" and thus save them from insanity and probably from hell itself.

Bastards
(Also see Children; Family; Law)

Leonardo da Vinci was called by his brothers, "The kitchen maid's bastard." This great artist, scientist and anatomist was revolted by anything connected with birth.

Jean Jacques Rousseau, author of *The Social Contract* and other celebrated humanist books, had all five of his "love children" put in orphan asylums.

Children should be obedient to their fathers, at first of necessity, and afterward from gratitude.　　　　　　—JEAN JACQUES ROUSSEAU

Lord Chesterfield's famous letters were to a bastard son.
　　Among those letters: "A man of sense only trifles with them [women], humors them, flatters them. But he neither consults them nor trusts them, though he often makes them believe that he does."

Anne, Queen Mother of Austria, bestowed the abbey of Maubuisson upon the Princess Louise-Hollandine, whose niece, many years later, wrote: "The Abbess has had so many bastards that she swore by 'this belly that has borne fourteen children.'"

Alexandre Dumas, the father *(Three Musketeers, Count of Monte Cristo),* and Alexandre Dumas, his son *(The Lady of the Camellias),* often lived together with their changing mistresses.
　　The son was illegitimate (as the son's mother was). The father was the son of a black slave girl and a French marquis.

Among other "natural" children: philosophers d'Alembert, Epictetus and Erasmus; artists Giorgione and Delacroix; writers Boccaccio and Aretino.

Alexander Hamilton was rumored to be George Washington's son, but definitely was not. A Scottish peddler was his father.

Amandine Aurore Lucie Dupin, who renamed herself George Sand, wrote celebrated novels, had many lovers (including Frédéric Chopin) and scandalized her name by wearing trousers, came from an almost unbroken line of bastards, which included the king of Poland (not an uncommon thing, for he was known to have accounted for at least two hundred "natural" children—some say twice that number).

Maurice de Saxe, the famous marshal of France, who was one of the king's bastards, had an affair with an actress, which resulted in the birth of a girl, Marie Aurore. She, under the protection of Madame la Dauphine of France, married the Count de Horne, himself fathered without benefit of clergy by Louis XV.

Three weeks later the count was killed in a duel and Marie married Claude Dupin who had been her aunt's lover. (Dupin had once fathered a child upon the celebrated Madame d'Epinay. That child was later made into an archbishop.)

The child of this union was called Maurice, after the aforesaid bastard son of the Polish king. This second Maurice met and impregnated a camp follower of the army, Sophie Delaborde, a "daughter of the people." Under extreme pressure, and at the very last moment, Maurice married Sophie, who then gave birth to a child who left her mark upon the turbulent world, namely, George Sand.

George Sand smoking a "hookah," drawn by her lover, Alfred de Musset.

Both Queen Mary and Queen Elizabeth I, who succeeded her, were "officially" called "bastards."

It was not until he had fathered her four children that Robert Burns married Jean Armour.

When the servant in Karl Marx's home became pregnant and was delivered of an infant, there were conjectures that Marx was the father. Others thought it to be his collaborator, Friedrich Engels. Still others believed that just as they had jointly authored the *Communist Manifesto,* both of them had had relations with the woman.

Benjamin Franklin's illegitimate son had an illegitimate son who had an illegitimate son.

One of the two "love children" of Isadora Duncan, the remarkable dancer and innovator, was fathered by Gordon Craig, the noted stage designer and producer. He himself was the illegitimate son of the illustrious Ellen Terry.

Both of Duncan's children were drowned when the car they were in slid down an embankment and into the river.

She herself was strangled to death by her scarf, which caught in the spokes of a wheel of the car in which she was riding.

Celibacy
(Also see Religion; Saints)

Of all the crimes of which the Emperor Elagabalus stood accused, it was his violation of a Vestal Virgin that finally provoked his assassination.

Virginity was idealized, had magical powers. When a hungry lion was turned loose on Thecla in the arena, it was said, he stopped short and then licked her feet in adoration of her purity.

No historical treasure, not even the Holy Grail, has been so highly appraised, or so zealously guarded, as the "maidenhead." Unlike

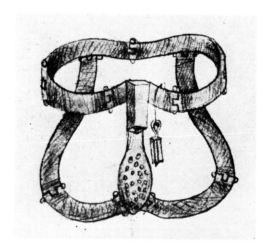

A fifteenth-century chastity belt—designed to keep all men away except, presumably, the husband who held the key to unlock it.

Venus, who was able to restore her virginity countless times simply by bathing in the sea, once a mortal maiden's virginity was lost, her reputation, marriageability and sometimes her life were lost as well.

So holy was the state of virginity regarded that one saint said that the only justification for the horrifying sexual act was that it resulted in more virgins being born.

There is a narrow passage in the crypt of Ripon Cathedral built by Odo, Archbishop of Canterbury, which was said to have been used to test whether young women were virgins or not. None but a virgin could squeeze through.

Many sects considered that the devil invented marriage (and sex).

Marriage has pains but celibacy has no pleasures.

—Samuel Johnson

In early times, when clergymen were forbidden to marry, they often lived with women without benefit of clergy.

There were also spiritual unions: live-in virgins—older women as well—who shared the homes of clergymen without carnal activities.

The Church of Spain finally decided, about A.D. 600, that the practice must end, and the females should be sold as slaves.

Jacques Jordaens,
Susanna and the Elders.

It was not because the two elders raped Susanna that they were put to death (though this was a crime), but because they falsely testified that she was not a virgin.

Since nuns were considered brides of Christ, medieval authorities declared that if a nun sinned carnally, she was guilty of *three* crimes: incest, sacrilege and adultery.

I could be content that we might procreate like trees, without conjunction, or that there were ways to perpetuate the world without this trivial and vulgar way of coition.   —SIR THOMAS BROWN

Saint Augustine prayed to God: "Give me chastity, but not yet!"

For the first three hundred years celibacy was not compulsory for the lower orders of the clergy.

In 1018 Pope Benedict VII declared that children of the clergy should be perpetual serfs of the church, and that their mothers were to be considered no higher than concubines.

And in 1073 the council in Rome declared that sex between priests and women was whoredom.

Martin Luther maintained that celibacy was invented by the devil; that celibacy itself is a cause of sin. (He said that he once personally wrestled with the devil; that he once threw an inkwell at him.)

"Whatever is a man must have a woman and whatever is a woman must have a man. . . . It is more necessary than sleeping and waking, eating and drinking, and emptying the bladder and the bowels."

This being so, said Luther, and God having commanded us to be fruitful and to multiply, "monks, priests and nuns are duty bound to forsake their vows whenever they find that God's ordinance to produce seed and to multiply is powerful and strong within them."

Suiting their actions to his words, Luther and Katharina von Bora, a nun, renounced vows of celibacy and married each other.

He suggested that sex should be indulged in only twice a week. (But he was forty years old when he married.)

Martin Luther and Katharina von Bora were reviled when they renounced vows of celibacy and married each other.

When a woman came to Cotton Mather, the celebrated American divine, and asked him to "couple" with her, he felt himself "consumed with the Foul Fire in the Male," but he rejected her advances.

Nowhere in the Old Testament is there any idealization of chastity as a permanent state.

The controversy over celibacy went on for over a thousand years, and is still not concluded.

In the Far East, the binding and crippling of the female infant's feet, which continued through childhood and adolescence, was part of the design to prevent her from being able to move beyond her own home without being carried, thus guarding against the possibility of any sexual adventures.

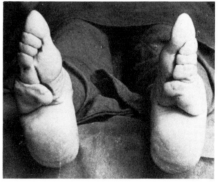

(Above) Distorted feet after a lifetime of binding.

(Left) The Chinese bound a female infant's feet, crippling her, and thereby prevented her from straying from home and the path of virtue.

In many areas of the Middle and Near East, immediate and visible and public proof of the bride's virginity was an integral element of the marriage ceremony. Following the wedding feast the couple would retire, while parents and guests surrounded the tent and awaited the outcome of the bedroom drama.

In due time, upon a prearranged signal, the parents of the bridegroom entered the tent and, if all went well, emerged waving the bloody sheet in proof of the bride's innocence.

Woe to the girl who failed to redden the sheet. The marriage itself was, ipso facto, at an end—which only began her troubles.

Fatima, Muhammad's favorite daughter, was believed by the faithful to be a virgin, though she had given birth to two sons.

The Crusaders, accompanied by prostitutes (thirteen thousand in a single year, according to one estimate), left their wives alone for long periods of time. To ensure their fidelity the wives were fitted with "chastity girdles," consisting of a metal framework with only a small opening for nonsexual functions, that closed over the hips by a lock. Only the husbands had the keys.

Or so they fondly believed.

Others said, "Love laughs at locksmiths."

Charms, Folklore and Magic

Among the South Slavs, a girl will dig up the earth from the footprints of the man she loves and put it in a flowerpot. Then she plants a marigold in the pot (a flower that is thought not to fade). And as its golden blossom grows and blooms and never fades, so shall her sweetheart's love grow and bloom, and never, never fade. Thus the love spell acts on the man through the earth he treads on.

Capture a rhinoceros, cut off its horn, crush it into a fine powder and put a pinch of it into a girl's bath. She will love you with a passion that passes all understanding.

Sex, unlike cigarettes, salt, sugar and stress, is good for one's hair.

Aristotle believed that when a cold north wind was blowing, a girl was most likely to be conceived. During warm winds boys were the more likely results. Which is why there was more sex performed by followers of Aristotle during nights the warm winds blew.

He also believed that menstrual blood was "half-cooked" semen.

There was a widespread belief among Pilgrims that a child conceived on a given day of the week would be born on the same day of the week. Some ministers balked, therefore, at baptizing a child born on the Sabbath, for it meant that the parents must have had carnal relations on the Sabbath, a grievous sin.

One minister, who was rigid in his adherence to this belief, was later faced with the embarrassment of his wife's giving birth on a Sabbath.

Minsky's Burlesque House was the foremost theater of its kind in America. Some devotees of the art were sufficiently stimulated to experience cures of certain ailments.

A number of times, when the performance was over and the audience had left, abandoned crutches would be found among the seats.

Minsky rejected the proposal to rename his theater "Minsky's Lourdes."

Steal a salt herring from the grocery store and eat it. Refrain from talking until after eating. The first man you dream about will marry you.

If you can walk around the block with your mouth full of water, you will marry this year.

Put an egg on the fire and sit down for an hour. The egg will sweat and the wind will howl, the dogs will bark and the geese will holler, and the man you are going to marry will come in and turn the egg around.

If the egg bursts open, you may never marry.

If when going up the stairs you stumble, it is a sign you will marry. The closer to the top you stumble, the sooner the marriage.

The Marquise de Montespan was charged with going to the notorious sorceress, Voisin, for love philters and charms to make Louis XIV more amorous. Later she tried to poison the king and her rival, Fontanges.

When a cat washes its face, the first person it looks at will be the first married.

If you want to sneeze but can't, someone loves you but dares not say so.

To make a girl fall madly in love with you, hide the dried tongue of a turtledove in her room.

The wedding ring, symbolic of the pledge of fidelity and of unity, was placed on the so-called ring finger and still is, because ancient "science" believed it discovered in that finger a nerve communicating directly to the heart.

Roy Lichtenstein, *The Ring.*

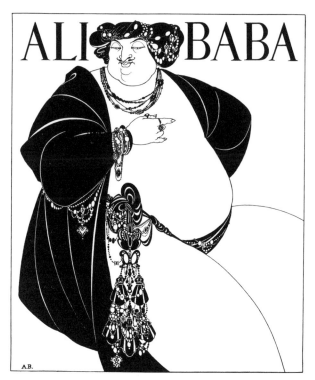

Aubrey Beardsley, *Ali Baba,* from the *Arabian Nights.*

Richard Burton, the extraordinary explorer, scientist and linguist (who translated the *Arabian Nights* and was bitterly attacked for its "pornography" by the English and American press), noted that pregnant Hindu women were taken to a special shrine and seated upon a particular lingam with the hope that the fetus, if female, would miraculously be changed into a male.

Richard Burton, on the benefits of marriage to the Moslem male: "The first kiss that the bridegroom gives is equal to 180 years of worship. It also enables him to escape the torments of the tomb, causes a light to be shed over his grave and procures the ministerings of eighty angels."

In 1810, a case was reported of a girl who, to rid herself of a rival, gathered up some of the sand the rival had walked on and, holding it over a fire, caused the rival to shrivel up and die.

Nymphs, naiads, lorelei, sirens and other "elementals," anxious to acquire a soul by intercourse with humans, sometimes seduce humans and sleep with them.

Sometimes demons assault individuals and have sexual congress with them against their will—even in public.

How to tell if he (or she) loves you: Pluck petals from a daisy and intone:

> He loves me,
> He loves me not,
> He loves me,
> He loves me not
> Etc., etc., etc.

until all the petals are gone. The last petal tells the tale. (Since this method is infallible, it does not do any good to cheat.)
    Another version:

> He loves me,
> He don't.
> He loves me,
> He won't.
> He would if he could,
> But he can't.

Advice to young maidens: Wear a four-leaf clover in the heel of your left shoe. You will marry the first man you meet.

Hang a four-leaf clover over the doorway; the first man to enter will be your husband.

Make a love potion by drying and crushing to a powder the web of a gander's foot. A pinch of this in a girl's coffee will cause her to love you forever.

A long time ago—a very long time ago—chicken soup was regarded as an aphrodisiac.

But the king was merciful because she was the mother of most of his children.

Nero, sleepless after having had his mother killed, tried by magical rites to summon up his mother's spirit so that he might be forgiven by her.

Shunammitism: an ancient belief that the scent of young people has a healing and rejuvenating effect on the old. It is named after the virgin of Shunem, Abishag, who was brought to the bed of King David, as he lay dying, in a vain effort to revive him.

Let me smell for very long, the odor of your hair. . . . My soul voyages upon its aroma as that of other men on the wings of music."

—BAUDELAIRE

Joris Karl Huysmans spoke of the "odorous melody of beasts and woods"—and was transported by the scent of a woman's underarms.

Children
(Also see Bastards; Family; Law)

From a news report in December 1979: Longview, Texas: The Reverend Charles Holland walked by the Nativity scene in front of his church and heard the sound of a baby's cries coming from the manger.

"My initial impression was that they had added this as an effect," Mr. Holland said. "Then I realized it was not from a tape but was for real."

Close behind the manger, in a small cardboard box, "sure enough, there was a little baby boy, without clothes, covered with a crib sheet doubled a couple of times," said Mr. Holland, who is pastor of the First Baptist Church.

An unsigned, handwritten note found along with the baby read: "I'm Timothy. Please take care of me."

Suffer, little children . . .

The legal skirmish over Ian Eaton's "regularly scheduled visit" to his firefighter mother's breast was decided in Ian's favor.

From a news report March 31, 1980: Linda Eaton, an Iowa City firefighter who was suspended for breast-feeding her baby at the firehouse, was awarded $2,000 in damages and $26,400 to cover lawyer's fees yesterday by the Iowa Civil Rights Commission.

Miss Eaton, the city's first female firefighter, was also awarded $145 for two days pay she lost in January 1979, when she was sent home from work for nursing her son, Ian, during unassigned work time in a women's locker room. She filed a sex-discrimination complaint after Fire Chief Robert Keating suspended her, citing an unwritten policy forbidding "regularly scheduled family visits."

The "regularly scheduled visit" of the infant to its mother's breast was felt not to constitute a violation.

From a news report March 19, 1980: A young couple was arrested for arranging to sell their fourteen-month-old son and their 1969 Dodge for a 1977 black and silver Corvette automobile.

Anna Sforza, aged three, was affianced to Alfonso d'Este, who was newborn and was carried to the ceremony by a chamberlain.

When a male infant was born in Sparta a health commission decided whether the baby was likely to grow up to be a healthy soldier. If not, they ruled that it be thrown into the Gorge of Taygetus.

From the records of the Diocese of Chester, England, in 1561: John Rigmarden, aged three, was married to a bride, aged five. Borne in the arms of a clergyman, he had to be coaxed into repeating the marriage words. When he indicated that he'd had enough, the priest said that after only a little more he could go out and play.

In one of his short stories, Anatole France gives us a six-year-old orphan, Jessy, who has been brought to her scholarly old uncle to live with. A few days later, she says, "Uncle you are old and you are ugly, but I love you and you must love me."

"Why must I love you?"

"Because I am little," she replies.

France, childless, told this story to express his feeling for the defenseless, especially children. After his longtime mistress died, he married her maid and lived happily with her until she died.

His own mother had been illegitimate.

Colonial America

In 1720, Lord Cornbury, first cousin to Queen Anne, was appointed governor of New York and was addressed as His High Mightiness. At his first formal banquet he delivered a eulogy to his wife's ears and required all the gentlemen to file past her and feel her ears for themselves.

Among other peccadilloes, His High (drunken) Mightiness, dressed in his wife's clothes, would pounce upon various male citizens and fondle their ears. He also stole money from the colony's treasury.

Eventually, the patience of the colonists had worn thin and they succeeded in lodging him in debtor's prison, where, it was said, the jailor successfully defended his ears *and* his honor against His (former) High Mightiness.

George Cooke, *The Coming of the Maidens.* From Brideswell, a notorious British jail, came wives for American colonists.

Wives for the settlers in Virginia were obtained from a number of sources, including criminals (mostly for prostitution) from Brideswell— the most notorious of prisons. The planters were required to pay as much as 150 pounds of tobacco ("of good leafe") for one of these "brides of Brideswell."

Between 1700 and 1770 over ten thousand women from England's jails were sent to the American colonies—mostly to the South.

In the main, these ancestors of our "First Families of Virginia" proved to be good wives, as honest and moral as those from any other background.

In 1619 a captain of a ship transported 144 single women to Virginia and sold them to the colonists. These women came to the captain voluntarily, in answer to his advertisement, but other captains kidnapped young women and transported them to the colonies against their will.

The Wedding of Pocahontas. John Rolfe insisted that it was not lust that motivated him but rather his need to save her soul for God.

Pocahontas, who saved John Smith's life, was a joyous young girl and a favorite of the English. She was one of twelve daughters and twenty sons of the great chief Powhatan—by his several wives. He gave refuge to many runaway settlers who preferred living among his tribesmen—and tribeswomen—to their own colony. John Rolfe pleaded with Sir Thomas Dale, the marshal of the colony, to be allowed to marry Pocahontas, saying that it was not because of any "unbridled carnal affection," but to Christianize her "for the glory of God and for my own salvation."

She agreed, although she was already married to a young Indian. Her father agreed, thinking it might help the cause of peace.

Rolfe took Pocahontas (now renamed Rebecca) to England, where she was presented to the king and was praised by all.

A few days before she was to return to Virginia, she died.

This and possibly one other marriage (between Pocahontas's sister and a settler) were the only intermarriages of Indian and white. But there were countless cases of sexual relations—some forced, others voluntary.

An indentured woman was not allowed to marry during her term of service. If she became pregnant, a year was added to her service.

Boatloads of women were sent to New Orleans from France. Whether the women were from brothels or were respectable, they invariably found husbands.

The king's representative in Canada wrote to Paris: "With wives I will anchor the roving *coureurs de bois* with sturdy colonists. Send me wives for the Canadians. They are running in the woods after Indian girls."

George Washington's ancestor John, the first American Washington, married Anne Gerard, even though she was accused of running a whorehouse. He was her third husband.

When Anne died, John married her sister, who stood accused of being the town whore as well as the mistress of the colonial governor.

In the very first years of "the American experiment," one Thomas Morton, Gentleman, was expelled and sent back to England for giving firearms to Indians in return for sexual favors from Indian women.

Writing in 1707, Virginia's first native-born historian, Robert Beverly, reported that it was the custom of the Indians to entertain important visitors, Indian or English, with feasts and dancing until bedtime, "when a brace of beautiful virgins are chosen to wait upon him for his particular refreshment. They esteem it a breach of hospitality not to submit to his desires."

Beverly suggested that intermarriage between Indians and whites would have prevented the bloodshed that bedeviled America. Years later, Patrick Henry proposed a law (which was never put into practice) encouraging such unions and granting a bounty for each child resulting therefrom.

A Virginian court heard the complaint of one husband that his wife refused to have sex with him. She charged that his practices were cruel and revolting to her. The court decreed that her pleasure or her abhorrence was immaterial, and ordered her to submit to her husband. After all, it was the holy duty of the woman to bear children. Her response was to slay her five-year-old daughter to keep the child from experiencing a fate similar to her own.

She was hung for her crime, the first woman in the colony so punished.

When the Pequot Indians were effectively destroyed, a number of the remaining young Indian women were divided up among the soldiers to be used as concubines. But for coupling with an Indian, Goodwife Mendame of Duxbury was sentenced "to be whipt at a cart's tayle through the town's streets and to wear a badge with the capital letter *A* on her left sleeve, and if found without it, to be burned in the face with a hot iron."

In colonial Connecticut, bachelors were fined one pound a week, unless they had explicit authority to live alone.

In old New England if a child was born less than nine months after marriage, some courts fined the husband or had him whipped, while they put the wife in stocks for their "filthy dalliance."

During "starving time" in Virginia, a man killed his wife, "salted her and ate her," for which he was executed.

Among other crimes in Virginia for which the penalty in those harsh times was death: adultery, rape and sodomy.

Men who were guilty of seduction could be pilloried, whipped, branded on their cheeks, made to pay a sum of money to the girl's father and ordered to marry her. Any combination of these penalties was possible in the early years of New England.

Kissing one's wife in public was reason enough to be put in stocks.

In *The Anatomie of Abuses,* Philip Stubbes asserted that on May Day celebrations, no more than one third of the maidens who went into the woods came out "undefiled."

"What clipping, kissing, smooching and unclean handling!"

Thomas S. Noble,
Witch Hill or *The Salem Martyr.*

The Salem witch-hunting madness resulted in the death of thirty-two people and two dogs.

Perhaps the most revealing case to the modern mind is that of the innkeeper Bridget.

A witness testified that he rented a room in her inn and retired for the night, bolting the windows and the doors securely.

Nevertheless, in the middle of the night he awakened to find Bridget standing naked beside his bed. Realizing that none but a witch could have entered the room, he made ready to defend his honor. He drew his sword from its scabbard, but she grasped the naked sword in her hands and broke it in half.

Defenseless, he was compelled to submit to her lust.

She was hung for her witchery, and the inn fell into more godly hands.

John Hancock, whose signature is so dramatically placed on the Declaration of Independence, was both the landlord and the lover of Dorcas Griffiths. Preparing to marry another, John evicted Dorcas from both bed and house.

Later, she became the mistress of a captain in the British army.

Of two hundred persons admitted to the Congregational church in Groton, Massachusetts, between 1761 and 1775, about one third confessed to having engaged in premarital sex, equally divided between men and women.

A woman having children without marriage could be whipped, branded, fined. If she did not know who the father was, the child could be taken away from her and apprenticed to a tradesperson.

Governor Prence—in 1640—haled Arthur Howland before the court and had him fined stiffly for paying court to his daughter Elizabeth without his consent. Arthur persisted for seven years and was fined again and again until finally the governor relented and the marriage took place.

Among the earliest court decisions in Plymouth, Massachusetts, John Till was fined and lashed for "slandering his dame, saying he was going home to lye with her."

John Hews and Jone, his wife, adjudged to sit in the stocks because they said Jone conceived "with child by him before they were publicly married."

"Likewise John Thorp and Alice, his wife."

A youth was convicted of sodomy, or "bestiality," in Scituate in 1641 "according to ye law, Leviticus 20:15" (the Pilgrims didn't believe that defendants should be tortured to force a confession "except for grievous crimes when the magistrates may proceed so farr to bodily torments as racks, hot irons, etc.").

Communal Love

Herodotus wrote that the Agathyrsi have wives in common, "so that they may all be brothers and not envy or hate one another."

Socrates, in Plato's *Republic,* proposed a state in which the nuclear family would be destroyed. "Men and women are to live in common houses and meet at common meals. None of them will have anything especially his or her own. . . . They will be brought up together and will associate at gymnastic exercises. And so they will be drawn by a necessity of their natures to have intercourse with each other. Necessity is not too strong a word, I think. . . .

"And the wives of our guardians are to be in common, and their children are to be common, and no parent is to know his child, or any child his parent."

Sir Thomas More wrote that families could exist under a communal arrangement, but if there was an excess of children they ought to be distributed to families that had too few.

In his *Utopia,* the woman is shown naked to the suitor, and he to her, that they may be satisfied that there are no blemishes or deformities.

It is said that More himself showed his two naked daughters, as they were sleeping, to Sir William Roper, who was then able to make an intelligent choice.

According to Joseph Smith, founder of the Church of Jesus Christ of Latter Day Saints (Mormons), polygamy was sanctioned by God to Abraham, Isaac, Jacob and Solomon and therefore was a valid, sanctified mode of family life.

"If any man espouse a virgin, and desire to espouse another, and the first give her consent . . . then he is justified; he cannot commit adultery."

He convinced his reluctant wife, Emma, that she would be condemned by God if she did not consent to his additional marriages.

Brigham Young, who succeeded Joseph Smith, told the Mormons in Salt Lake City that Lowell, Massachusetts, had fourteen thousand more women than men, who "live and die in a single state and are forgotten." And because these women were not fulfilling the purpose for which God had created them, he urged that two thousand Mormon males should go there and "take to themselves seven women apiece."

Nothing, however, came of these heroic plans.

In the spring of 1854, Brigham Young had nine children born to his household in a single week.

In one of his sermons: "I have noticed that a man who has but one wife . . . soon begins to wither and dry up, while a man who goes into plurality looks fresh, young and sprightly."

They denied Jesus was celibate and cited that when He rose from the dead He first appeared to Mary, Martha and Mary Magdalene—not to his Apostles.

Mark Twain visited the Mormon community in Salt Lake City in 1861 and was struck by the "ungainly and homely" women. "The man who married one of them does an act of Christian charity which entitles him to the applause of mankind, not their harsh censure, and the man that married sixty of them has done a deed of openhanded generosity so sublime that the nations should stand uncovered in his presence and worship in silence."

In one such commune, John D. Lee was married to sixteen women and fathered sixty-five children. One of his wives, dissatisfied with him, asked for a divorce and permission to marry his eldest son by his first wife. Lee agreed and performed the ceremony himself.

John Warren headed a community on Long Island, New York, which he called "Modern Times," in which *there were no laws whatsoever.* Everyone performed as much work in the community workshops as he voluntarily wished to and took what he felt was needed for himself and family. No marriage laws were forced on members, and "a man may have two wives, or a woman two husbands, or a dozen each, for aught I care. . . . *Everyone has a perfect right to do everything."* So long as

MIRIAM WORKS	MARY ANN ANGELL	LUCY DECKER	HARRIET COOK
CLARA DECKER	CLARISSA CHASE ROSS	EMILY DOW PARTRIDGE	EMMELINE FREE
MARGARET PIERCE	SUSAN SNIVELY	MARTHA BOWKER	ZINA DIANTHA HUNTINGTON
NAAMAH KENDEL JENKINS CARTER	LUCY BIGELOW	ELIZA ROXEY SNOW	ELIZA BURGESS
HARRIET BARNEY	AMELIA FOLSOM	MARY VAN COTT	ANN ELIZA WEBB

Twenty of Brigham Young's twenty-seven wives. Only one, the last, divorced him.

it was voluntary, Warren believed that the pressure of social sanction would keep members from doing anything harmful to others. (The panic of 1857 destroyed the economic basis for the colony, which was then disbanded.)

John H. Noyes established communities in which every male was theoretically married to all the females. The women also were permitted to engage in sexual intercourse with as many men as they wished.

He claimed that sex was practiced in heaven as on earth, and that God approved. "To be ashamed of the sex organs is to be ashamed of God's workmanship."

The discovery of "continence" in the sex relationships, interpreted by Noyes as the ability to have sex without emission, was described by an enthusiastic admirer as "surpassing that of the steam engine and the electric telegraphy."

A celibate community known as the Women's Commonwealth was led by Martha MacWhirter and was composed of twenty-four women in a Bible class in Balton, Texas. Martha convinced them to leave their husbands and to form a commune in 1876. They resolved never to marry again. They were financially successful, but were harassed by rowdies and therefore moved to the District of Columbia.

The project lasted until 1906 when it was disbanded.

Jemima Wilkinson founded the New Jerusalem community in western New York in 1798. Her followers, known as "Jemimakins," believed that she was divinely inspired to establish a communist society based on celibacy. When one of them became pregnant, Jemima angrily suggested that the child be named "Abomination."

A Masai may marry as many wives as he can pay for. If he is rich there will be a separate hut for each wife.

The first wife is the chief wife and rules the household.

The young warriors and young girls live together in a separate establishment managed by the young men's mothers until the males are old enough to marry—between twenty-seven and thirty years of age.

Shakers, a celibate religious community.

The United Society of Believers in Christ's Second Appearing (known generally as the Shakers) practiced celibacy. The basis for their beliefs and practices was the fact that Adam and Eve lived a life of bliss until lust for each other appeared. Their leader was Ann Lee, who scolded her own mother for her "carnal acts of indulgence" with her father.

A similar chaste sect—the Rappites—was established by George Rapp in 1804 in Harmony, Pennsylvania. (Byron wrote a satiric poem about them.)

Rapp believed that Christ had no sexual organs. His followers believed that they could even share the same beds with their spouses and not be tempted.

In modern times, there are some utopian communities in which there is total sexual permissiveness; husbands, wives and lovers being shared at will. There are, however, other communal groups in which the nuclear family is the guiding principle.

There are a few communes based on homosexual relationships exclusively.

Courtesans
(Also see Prostitution)

Hetairae: highly cultivated courtesans of ancient Greece, who were celebrated for their beauty, intelligence and talent. (The word itself means "companion.") A hetaira could therefore be more sexually, aesthetically and intellectually exciting to the recipient of her favors.

Among the most famous of them was Aspasia, of stunning beauty, who was the celebrated Pericles' lover. She gave lectures in philosophy and rhetoric (Sophocles said that he studied rhetoric with her). Violently in love with her, Pericles divorced his wife and lived openly with her. His enemies charged her with impiety, being a procuress, as well as other such crimes. She was tried before a huge jury of Athenians.

Pericles was her counsel. He wept as he defended her. A renowned orator, he secured her acquittal; but it was at the cost of his reputation and of his power.

Lais, pupil of Aspasia and a hetaira of extraordinary beauty and charm, conducted famous "feasts of love and reason" at her salon, where all the famous wits, philosophers and political figures forgathered regularly and, as eighteen centuries later in the Court of Eleanor of Aquitaine, where complex questions about love were propounded and presumably solved.

Later, when Lais rejected the attentions of Vasileas, the high priest of Eleusis, he caused her to be arrested. At a famous trial, where Diogenes and others came to her defense (included among these were hundreds of poor people whom she had helped), she was acquitted, to the joy of the multitude.

Lais turned down Demosthenes, the great orator, spurning his offer of the equivalent of five thousand dollars for one night of love, but yielded to the ragged Diogenes for nothing.

In her will she asked that her mirror be buried with her.

Alexander ceded his mistress, Thais, to General Ptolomaeus, who became king of Egypt, making Thais his queen.

Hetaira

Athenian youths and Hetairae.

Phryne, believed by all Athens to be the most beautiful woman in history, and who was the model for Praxiteles' marvelous statues of Venus, was arrested and brought to trial for impiety.

In a single, swift gesture, her defense counsel, Hyperedes, pulled her flowing robe from her. As she stood there nude, Hyperedes demanded of the jury whether such a heavenly body could be guilty of impiety. Was it not a contradiction in terms? The jury, Athenian to the core, needed no other evidence of her innocence.

A slave girl, Cenis, became secretary to Antonia, the sister-in-law of the Roman emperor Tiberius. When she became mistress to Vespasian, Antonia freed her. When Vespasian became emperor, he married her.

Xerxes took a Milesian prostitute, Thargelia, with him as his mistress when he invaded Greece. He then used her as an emissary to the court at Thessaly. She succeeded so well there in her negotiations that the king married her.

Charles II shared one of his mistresses, Lady Castlemaine, with several of his friends. She threw them all over—for a time—because of her fascination with a handsome tightrope dancer.

It was an ancient custom for the displaced favorite of the French king to wait upon and even help dress her successor. Louise de la Vallière was thus forced to act as maid to Mme. Montespan when she was succeeded as mistress to the "Sun King," Louis XIV.

Many years later the king's fancy attached itself to the young Mlle. de Fontanges, who made the fatal error of demanding that Mme. Montespan now serve her. It wasn't long before de Fontanges died of a "mysterious ailment," which all France understood to mean that Montespan had used poison to avoid the ignominy of serving the new favorite.

When Mme. Montespan died, her children, fathered by Louis XIV, were prevented from attending her funeral because she was in disgrace as a witch and a murderer. The children had been made into dukes and princes by then.

Mme. de Montespan poisoned her successor.

Mme. de Pompadour.

As mistress of Louis XV, Mme. Pompadour was to rule the taste of France for twenty years. When she died, alone and poverty-stricken, the king, staring out of the window as the funeral carriage passed by in the rain, merely said, "The poor marquise has bad weather."

Mme. de Castiglione asked 1 million francs of an English lord for one night of love. He agreed. It was the price, not the performance, that was noteworthy, according to intimates of both parties to the contract.

When the fateful year 1000 came and went without the widely expected "coming," Rome gave itself over to unrestrained sensuality. It became the heyday of the great courtesans, who had enormous influence over kingdoms and bishoprics alike. It became known as the "pornocratic" epoch.

When the famous author Colette was eighty, she sighed and said, "Oh, to be fifty-eight and desired."

The equally famous Ninon de Lenclos, when *she* was eighty, was still going strong. Among the stories told of her:

A young, attractive man, seeking the ultimate favor of this fabled beauty, was told that he would have to wait until midnight of a certain day.

The day came, the church bells sounded twelve, and true to her word, Ninon introduced the young lover to unimaginable delights.

Later, he asked why she had put him off until this particular time. She said that at that exact hour she became eighty years old, and that she could think of no sweeter way to usher in her eightieth birthday than in his strong young arms.

Ninon conducted a famous salon where the wit and beauty of Paris gathered to do her homage. The extraordinary Queen Christine of Sweden said that she was the only woman in Europe worth knowing.

Among her lovers she numbered the greatest of all French statesmen, Cardinal de Richelieu (who could shed diplomatic tears at will); Marshal Maurice de Saxe, the celebrated epigrammatist; La Rochefoucauld; Prince Condé; and other luminaries too numerous to mention.

Among her conquests were the husband, son *and* grandson of the famous Mme. de Sévigné. (Of the son, she remarked that he had "a soul of boiled beef, a body of damp cardboard, and a heart like a pumpkin fricasseed in snow.")

The reason Christopher Columbus, then a widower, did not marry his mistress, Beatriz de Harana, was that it would not have advanced his career, she being the daughter of peasants. But he did provide handsomely for her and their son in his will "for the discharge of my conscience, because it weigheth much on my mind."

There was another Beatriz, whom he met while his fleet put in at Gomera, in the Canary Islands, while on his way to the New World. She had been maid of honor to Queen Isabella, but, worried about Ferdinand's intentions, the queen soon married her off to a conquistador who had been accused of murdering a rival. But he was pardoned when he agreed to take Beatriz as his bride and sail with her to the Canary Islands.

When Columbus met her there she had become a widow, still young and still beautiful. But before the romance could mature, Columbus had to resume his historic voyage, leaving a disappointed Beatriz behind.

They never met again.

Carpaccio, *Courtesans of Venice.* The Senate tried in vain to limit the splendor of prostitutes' costumes.

Fifteenth-century Flemish shield depicting romantic love,
the agonies and ecstasies of which were to be experienced
only outside the marriage relationship.

Courtly Love

The Crusaders left their wives alone for long periods of time. The troubadours came into being and sang their songs of romance to them, songs celebrating the agony of love.

The "romantic agony" was solidly based in the problems of sexual consummation. Even when a knight might have access to the lady (usually married to another), it was the ecstasy of refraining from the ultimate embrace that was celebrated in song and story. He who while nude could lie beside the equally nude loved one, quivering with desire and yet not follow nature's dictates, was a hero to the practitioners of the art of romantic love.

All the devotees of courtly love agreed that passion in the romantic sense could not exist between husband and wife because there was no problem of sexual gratification. They were, in fact, legally bound to engage in sexual intercourse; while the very essence of romantic love was the difficulty, even the impossibility, of such activity. Or, if it were achieved, it was at some terrible cost, including guilt, insanity and death. The greater the difficulty the greater the romantic agony.

Some cynics have asserted that these high-flown sentiments were often a mere cover-up for raw sexual lusts. Others, responding, pity the cynics for their inability to experience the highest form of passion.

Marie, Countess of Champagne and daughter of the famous Eleanor of Aquitaine, presided over one of the earliest courts of love, where complex and weighty questions bearing on the romantic agony were ventilated and solved. For example:

A knight complained that the lady he loved was pledged to another, but that she had promised that if she lost her lover she would then love him. Later, she *married* her lover and so, the complainant declared, she must now love him because the marriage canceled her and her husband's status as lovers.

After lengthy and complex argumentation, the queen declared that since romantic love cannot exist between husband and wife, the lady indeed had lost her lover and now must honor her vow to give her love to the complaining knight.

Since the time of the troubadours, tales, ballads and graceful questions were part of the conversations of the courts. For example: "Beau, sire, which would you prefer: that people spoke ill of your lady and that you found her good, or that she were well spoken of and that you should find her bad?" The strict conception of honor obliged a gentleman to answer, "I should prefer to hear her well spoken of and that I should find her bad."

Another example, "Does a lady, neglected by her lover, break faith by choosing another?"

A theme for the troubadour's song: "Which is more worthy: the agony or the ecstasy of love?"

The story is told of one Ulrich, who, to prove the sincerity of the sentiments he expressed to a lady in some verses he wrote, sent one of his fingers along with the poem.

A courtly French jongleur, when asked why he did not write more on love, said, "Love is only for the rich."

Courtship
(Also see Marriage)

In ancient Sparta, young males and females played games and danced nakedly together. Plutarch: "Appearing naked in their exercises and dancings were incitements to marriage, operating upon the young with the rigor and certainty, as Plato says, of love, if not of mathematics."

When Henry VII's queen died in 1503, he thought of marrying the young queen of Naples. To this end he sent three emissaries who were armed with twenty-four items about which they were to report to him. These involved her appearance, height, complexion, the length of her nose, size of her feet, color of hair, condition of her teeth, whether her fingers were slender or thick, her neck long or short, whether there were any blemishes on her body (their answer to this item was to recount a conversation with the queen's apothecary who assured them of her unblemished body) and so on.

Question number 16: "Item, to mark her breasts and paps, whether they be big or small."

Answer: "The queen's breasts be somewhat great and fully, and inasmuch as they were trussed somewhat high after the manner of the country, the which causeth her grace for to seem much the fullyer and her neck to be shorter."

In general, Henry seems to have been satisfied with the answers, except for question 24, dealing with the queen's finances. She was physically fit but fiscally wanting, and so the king remained a widower.

Somewhat later, a case was made for the queen of Castile, despite the fact that her embalmed former husband was her constant companion, even while traveling. (Henry was not enchanted.)

Among the old Scots, "handfasting" was a contract between two Highland chiefs, by which it was agreed that the heir of one should live with the daughter of the other as her husband for twelve months and a day. If the woman produced a child or became pregnant during that time, the marriage became good in law. Otherwise, both parties were free to handfast or marry elsewhere.

In a case in London, a widow created something of a record when, her husband having died one midnight, she called upon the draper to measure her for widow's weeds early next morning. Her measurements must have had a feverish effect upon the draper and perhaps his upon her, for they were married before noon on that very day.

"Bundling" in New England was also called "tarrying" and referred to the practice of a young man being allowed to lie side by side in bed with a young woman, fully dressed. Often a board separated the two conversationalists. Sometimes the female's blanket would be sewed together.

The practice was imported from cold European countries as a

way of saving fuel and, as a fringe benefit, of expediting the courtship. Ironically, it was brought to the New World by the Puritans.

John Adams, no bundler himself, gave qualified approval: "I cannot entirely disapprove of bundling."

A heated defense by an old gentleman (in 1720): "What is the use of sitting up all night and burning out fire and lights when you could just as well kiver up and keep warm? Why, damn it, there wasn't half as many bastards then as there are now."

To the same effect, a stanza in a long poem defending the practice:

> Since in a bed a man and a maid
>   May bundle and be chaste
> It doth no good to burn up wood.
>   It is a needless waste.

On the other hand: a poem of twenty-seven stanzas, ending:

> Down deep in hell there let them dwell,
> And bundle on that bed;
> There burn and roll without control,
> Till all their lusts are fed.

In old New England, the Reverend Edward Taylor writes to Elizabeth Fitch in 1671: "For you have made my Breast the cabinet of your affections . . . I know not how to use a finer comparison to set out my love than to compare it to a Golden Ball of Pure Fire rowling up and down my Breast, from which there flies now and then a spark like a Glorious Beam from the body of the Flaming Sun."

Elizabeth, duly impressed, married the fervent minister, and from that Golden Ball of Pure Fire there issued forth thirteen lovely children.

In the "shivaree," a custom in the Midwest (and elsewhere), the friends of the bridal pair gather secretly around the house the couple have retired to and make a tremendous din with cowbells, washboards, tin dishpans and the like.

When the couple emerges they invite everyone in for food, wine and more festivities, which last until daylight.

The practice of noisemaking, including tying tin cans to the vehicles bearing the bridal party away, originated in times when it was felt necessary to drive away evil or jealous spirits.

Overheard in Central Park, New York City: "I met my wife in fiscal '63 while sitting in the boardroom of Merrill Lynch."

While sexual relations among young unmarried people within any given collective (kibbutz) in Israel do take place, marriage almost never does.

The fact that from infancy on, through childhood, adolescence and young adulthood, they play, study, work and dwell together, deprives the relationship of the elements of adventure, of mystery and, hence, of romance. Simultaneously, it seems to engender an incestuous sense that effectively inhibits the idea of marriage within that kibbutz.

A few actual letters from those seeking dates from one computer dating service:

"I have filled out my son's application because no one knows him better than his mother."

"According to a survey, 20 percent of college girls engage in premarital sex. This is the group I am primarily interested in."

"All I want is a nice Jewish boy who is in his father's business."

Marriage by capture: a ritual that descended from primitive times, when the victorious armies carried off by force the women of the defeated foe.

The agreement having been made between the parties, the girl was then supposed to run for her life and/or freedom, but was captured—or "kidnapped"—and brought "struggling" and screaming to the groom's house.

Other versions among various tribes: It was the bridegroom's friends who "ambushed" the bride and carried her to his home—or placed her on a horse beside the bridegroom, who then dashed off with her.

It is believed that the modern practice of carrying the bride across the threshold is a survival of the ancient custom of marriage by capture.

Among the Bushmen of South Africa, when young people marry, a feast takes place with the families of both participants present.

Near the end of the feast, the groom pretends to drag the bride away, causing a "fight" in which the groom is hit by sticks. The couple is then allowed to escape—but not without objects being flung after them.

The throwing of rice, confetti and the like is believed to have originated in such rituals. Also the practice of throwing rice at the bridal pair was intended to ensure good luck and fertility.

In India, some tribes draw blood from the hands of the bride and groom and mix their blood into dishes of boiled rice and milk. Each then eats from the dish containing the other's blood.

It was an ancient practice among the Indians of North America for the bridal couple to eat cooked corn from the same dish. This in itself was considered among some tribes to constitute a marriage bond.

On Madagascar, the couple alternately eat food from the same dish, symbolizing their unity.

In ancient France, the bride stepped on and broke an egg on the threshold of her new home to ensure good luck.

Gypsies, among others, break a dish (or glass) as part of the wedding ceremony.

> That man that hath a tongue, I say, is no man,
> If with this tongue he cannot win a woman.
>
> —SHAKESPEARE, *Two Gentlemen of Verona*

On the other hand:

> They that are rich in words, in words discover
> That they are poor in that which makes a lover.
>
> —SIR WALTER RALEIGH

Divorce
(Also see Family; Law)

Julius Caesar divorced Pompeia even though nothing was proved against her, because "Caesar's wife must be above suspicion."

The virtuous Cato, after having been divorced from Marcia, felt no shame in taking her back when her private fortune was augmented by that of Hortensius, whom she had married and lost in the interval.

In ancient Rome, at one time, a simple declaration by either husband *or* wife was sufficient to dissolve the marriage.

If a soldier was away too long, the wife could get a divorce.

Charlemagne decreed that a man might have only one wife and that he could not divorce her—only separate from her.

But then he himself put his first wife aside and married several times thereafter.

Harriet Douglas, sister-in-law of President James Monroe, divorced her husband and, to demonstrate the finality of the action, had her marriage bed sawed in half. She made two strange-looking sofas out of the halves.

(A century later, in Los Angeles, when a judge decreed that a house in which a divorced couple had lived belonged to both of them, the enraged husband sawed the entire house in two and offered his ex-wife the choice of either half.)

Christina Onassis, daughter of Aristotle Onassis and possibly the richest woman in the world, fell in love with a Russian Communist (presumably devoted to the idea of the elimination of capitalism), married him and moved into his two-room flat (which also contained his mother). She expressed herself as perfectly happy with the arrangement, but divorced him a year later, giving him a freighter as a going-away present. Whether this was sufficient consolation for him has not been disclosed, though it is said that his mother is happier because she regained sole kitchen privileges of the flat.

When, during the divorce proceedings, sensational reports appeared to the effect that Christina's husband was a spy who used his relationship to Christina to gain information about oil reserves, naval installations and so forth, she replied: "What do you think we spoke about in bed? Oil?"

A full-page advertisement in the *New York Times* (March 11, 1980) began by declaring:

I WANT A GIRL

JUST LIKE THE GIRL

WHO DIVORCED DEAR OLD DAD.

Divorce only reassorts the couples: a very desirable thing when they are ill-assorted.   —GEORGE BERNARD SHAW

Heywood Broun, noting that many of the divorced people he knew were more friendly to one other than when they had been married, suggested that instead of a marriage ceremony people should start their lives together by going through a divorce ceremony.

It was the scandal of a divorce that effectively destroyed the one chance Ireland had of uniting the largely Protestant north and the Catholic south.

Charles Stewart Parnell was both architect and symbol of the unifying impulse. But when the beautiful Kitty O'Shea was sued for divorce and Parnell was named as her adulterous partner, the movement for unity collapsed.

Family
(Also see Marriage)

According to Caesar, at the time of the Roman conquest it was not unusual for several brothers or a father and his sons to have one wife among them in ancient Britain.

Lothar, the youngest son of Clovis, the Frankish king who was converted to Christianity, had seven wives and many concubines. His wife Ingund asked him to find a suitable husband for her sister, Aregund.

Later, Lothar to Ingund: "I sought a man wealthy and of good wit . . . but I have found none better than myself. Know, therefore, that I have taken her to wife, which I believe will not displease thee."

Ingund, we are assured, submitted with good grace to the arrangement.

A headstone in a New England cemetery:

> Here lies my daughter Charlotte
> Born a virgin, died a harlot.

Charlemagne, as the Holy Roman Emperor, forbade his children marrying because he wanted them with him. But he did not object to their affairs and he was fond of the children resulting from these unsanctified unions.

(That he was not opposed to marriage as such is proved by the fact that he married off, in one mass ceremony, all the widows of the barons who died in Spain to young men of his choice.)

Robert E. Lee, the commander of the Armies of the Confederacy, did not forbid his daughters to marry, and yet they remained single. Some people felt that his adoring daughters felt that no man could equal their handsome and charismatic father.

Charles V's only mistress, Barbara Blomberg, a prostitute from Regensburg, bore a son who later demanded she enter a convent, for her loose and extravagant way of living threatened his hard-won position as governor-general of the Netherlands.

By a most extraordinary coincidence, four centuries later, Hitler's minister of war, whose name was also Blomberg, was dismissed from his post because it was discovered that he had married a prostitute. Though the names were the same, there was no relationship, the general being from an aristocratic Prussian family. (His name was preceded by a "von.")

Bacon said, "He that hath wife and children hath given hostages to freedom, for they are impediments to great enterprises."

Andrew Carnegie promised his mother that he would not marry while she lived. Despite his millions (he got 400 million dollars from J. P. Morgan for his steel interest—equal to at least 5 billion in 1980 dollars), he kept his promise. Finally, when she died, he did marry. He was fifty-two years old.

When Edward Gibbon *(The History of the Decline and Fall of Rome)* wished to marry, his parents dissuaded him.

"I sighed as a lover, I obeyed as a son," he wrote.

Mrs. Richard Caton, the daughter of Charles Carroll of Carrollton (who had signed the Declaration of Independence), was the first American to marry off her daughters to English peers. They became the Duchess of Leeds, the Baroness Stafford and the Marchioness of Wellesley. In London they were referred to as the "Three American Graces."

Diana, Jessica, Deborah and Unity Mitford, the talented daughters of Lord and Lady Redesdale, developing in a widely—and wildly—divergent manner, created one sensation after another, especially in their marriages.

Diana married Sir Oswald Mosley, the Fascist leader who wanted England to imitate the Nazi state. They were both jailed for treason when war broke out.

Jessica, violently opposed to fascism, first married Winston Churchill's nephew, whose sympathies were Communist. After he died in the war, she married an American of similar views. Later, they both joined the Communist party, causing an international sensation and irreparable rifts among the sisters.

Deborah made the most traditional marriage—to the Duke of Devonshire.

Another sister, Unity, infatuated with Hitler, became a member of his entourage. Hitler described her as "the perfect Nordic type." She shot herself when the war broke out.

Various studies of the minds of murderers have shown that in most cases their lives have been notable for a lack of affectionate relations with their parents.

In the case of the assassin of President McKinley, it was considered significant that he was carrying an ordinary rubber baby "pacifier" with him—unused.

The circumstances of Lee Harvey Oswald having slept in the same bed as his mother until he was eleven years of age is thought to have been a clue to his violent and aberrant conduct.

James Earl Ray, Martin Luther King's murderer, was subjected to the harshest kind of cruelty and deprivation by a vicious father.

The father of Robert Kennedy's assassin had early abandoned his family.

Psychiatrists have adduced such facts in explanation, not in extenuation, of these crimes.

President McKinley's assassin carried an unused baby pacifier with him.

It was said of the Soong sisters (Ai-ling, Mei-ling and Ching-ling) that "one loved money"—Ai-ling, who married the banker H. H. Kung; "one loved power"—Mei-ling, who married Chiang Kai-shek, who ruled China as head of the Kuomintang; and the third "loved the people"— Ching-ling, who married Sun Yat-sen, the leader of the movement that transformed China into a republic.

The language of the Trobriand Islands, part of the Territory of Papua, has no word for "father" because until recent times the relationship between sex and conception was unknown to them. (For that reason descent was reckoned through the mother—matrilineally.)

Sex existed purely for pleasure, in their view, and when the missionaries came and taught them the facts of procreation the islanders were either amused or angry.

According to early Roman law (known as the law of the twelve tables), the head of the family was its absolute ruler. He could even sell its members into slavery if he was so disposed.

He could whip his wife and even condemn her to death if she was guilty of adultery or some other heinous offense.

When, later, women began to win some relief from these Draconian laws, Cato worried: "The moment they begin to be your equals they will be your superiors."

Mother love: The Talmud declares that since God could not be everywhere he created mothers. A revisionist: God *is* everywhere and everywhere He is He delights in creating mothers.

Hollywood
(Also see Actors)

Anita Loos *(Gentlemen Prefer Blondes),* one of Hollywood's earliest scriptwriters and one of its freest spirits, told this story to deflate the myth of Hollywood supersexuality:

A traveling salesman from Pittsburgh is accosted by a dazzling princess in Iran. When he gets back to Pittsburgh he tells his awestruck friends about the experience, describing the fabled gardens and palace to which the princess took him. Then the marvelous banquet, the perfumed bath, the gorgeous bed to which she led him. She slowly undresses her lovely body and then helps him do the same.

"And then? and then?" his pals asked him pantingly.

"Oh, well, then it was just like in Pittsburg."

According to the revelations by some women stars, it must have been even better in Pittsburgh than in Hollywood.

They are on record as being disillusioned with the lack of maleness in Hollywood males. Some of the most celebrated "romances" were a charade, designed to conceal from the public that the men involved were not what their screen images proclaimed them to be.

Things seem to be improving, however, at least according to the Niagara of books revealing "all"—including the secrets of the casting couch, bedroom, dressing room, fitting room, stateroom, bathroom, kitchen pantry, sauna, swimming pool, croquet lawn and even library, church and airplane cockpit.

When the Dominican dictator's son came to Hollywood and spent what some said was almost half the aid given to that country by the United States, a congressional committee took up the matter.

When the full extent of young Trujillo's largesse was disclosed (Rolls-Royces, chinchilla coats and so forth), Congressman Wayne Hayes characterized one beneficiary as "the most expensive courtesan since Pompadour."

Later, the congressman was compelled to resign when he was charged with misuse of office accounts by keeping his mistress on the payroll.

When filling out an application for a passport, Errol Flynn replied "sex" to the question of his occupation and "occupation" to the question of his sex.

When he was fifty years old (the year of his death) he claimed to have had fifteen thousand nights of sexual love. When it was remarked that he would have had to occupy every night of his life from the age of five, Flynn shrugged and said, "So—what's your problem?"

Fatty Arbuckle,
1920s sensation.

The Code: Some of the scandals were so messy (Fatty Arbuckle/ Virginia Rappe) and some of the films so raunchy that the film industry felt impelled to satisfy such critical agencies as the Legion of Decency by setting up a code to be administered by a "czar."

According to this code, there could be no more openmouthed kisses, nor could even a chaste kiss last for more than three seconds. No double beds could be shown, nor even twin beds if they were occupied by male and female—even if the occupants had been married from the year one.

Double entendres were enthusiastically blue-penciled; in fact, nothing indicating that the mating of men and women, like that of other species, remotely involving sex was allowed.

Curse words were verboten. It was a big thrill to hear Clark Gable use the word *damn* to Vivien Leigh in *Gone With the Wind* ("Frankly, my dear, I don't *give* a damn"). Or to see him take off his shirt, revealing no undershirt—just his manly chest, as he spoke to Claudette Colbert, with only a hanging sheet separating them!

Hollywood, "the dream factory of the world," became the graveyard of those dreams for many of its leading performers. For thousands of beautiful girls who were drawn there because they had won some local beauty contest or because people said they were "pretty enough to be in the movies," the experience was no better than a nightmare, many of them becoming call girls or, if they were lucky enough, returning home to marry the faithful hometown boy.

Marriages in Hollywood tended to be very temporary alliances. Barbara La Marr, one of the most beautiful and glamorous of stars, was married six times before she was twenty-five. Each successive marriage was to be final, "the perfect romance." At forty she was dead, a victim of narcotics.

So, too, Alma Rubens, often married (among her husbands, Ricardo Cortez), in and out of institutions for the insane, dead at thirty-four from an overdose.

Clara Bow, the "It" girl, was the most celebrated of the "jazz babies" of the Roaring Twenties. She reached out for love to anyone and everyone who lusted for her. When it was revealed that this included an episode in which most of the members of the U.S.C. football team were involved, she was pilloried in the press to such an extent that she suffered a series of mental breakdowns from which she never really recovered.

Clara Bow, the "It" girl, in *Dangerous Curves.*

Howard Hughes's love nests dappled the hills of Hollywood, providing shelter for aspiring actresses and booming times for the realtors. But too often the careers never materialized—indeed, the dour lover himself sometimes never materialized, either having forgotten the given lady altogether or because he was simply unable to find the time or energy to accommodate her.

He was an intrepid flyer but a cowardly lover, so that when one actress's husband—a muscular football player—caught them in flagrante delicto and then launched a few indignant blows at him, Hughes piteously pleaded for mercy. His two greatest fears: husbands and germs.

Homosexuality
(Also see Law; Manners and Morals)

Aristophanes is quoted by Plato in the *Symposium* as saying that only those young men who are devotedly homosexual develop into statesmen.

While admiring beauty in women, Socrates was also attracted to handsome young men. Some commentators believe that he resisted them sexually. They point to the example of his relationship with his stunningly attractive student Alcibiades, who tried to seduce him and failed, possibly the only such failure in his riotous young life. There are contrary opinions.

The sons of Constantine the Great (under whom Christianity became the official religion of the Roman Empire) declared homosexuality to be a capital offense.

Under Emperor Valentinian homosexuals were burned at the stake.

Louis XIV was advised that it was better for the army that some of the highborn officers were homosexuals, because otherwise they were reluctant to go on military campaigns. And even when they did so they most often left before or even during a battle in order to be with their lovers. But they went gladly into service when their lovers were with them.

Antonio Pollaiuolo, *Battle of the Naked Men.*

The famous Sacred Band of Thebes was composed entirely of three hundred homosexuals who acted as shock troops in war. In one extraordinary battle they fought until not one of them was left alive.

In Sparta, a trainee would have a mature lover who acted as his exemplar. It was felt that they both fought better when doing so side by side.

Aristotle made a case against sexual activities between males, but nevertheless said, "Love and friendship are found most and in the best form between men."

Serge Diaghilev, who discovered Vaslav Nijinsky and Leonide Massine and had become their lover, was "betrayed" by both of them when they married women.

Once, looking for a private secretary, he interviewed several young men. One of them, shown into Diaghilev's office, found him writing at his desk. Several minutes passed silently. Then, without looking at the applicant, Diaghilev said one word: "Undress."

Surprised, the young man did so. He stood there naked for a time until Diaghilev put a monocle into his eye, surveyed the young man's hairy body and said one more word: "Dress."

That was the end of it for the applicant.

"Monsieur," as Louis XIV's brother was known, was happiest dressed as a woman. He didn't ride horses for fear of spoiling his complexion. His mother and Cardinal Mazarin brought him up to be as much of a girl as possible so that he might not one day become a danger to his brother, challenging his rule.

Soon after Monsieur's marriage he told Madame that he preferred to sleep alone. He couldn't bear to be touched by her and if she did so by mistake he would shout curses at her. She was more than content to sleep alone. She was by then pregnant, thus having acquitted herself of her dynastic responsibilities.

"I never have had a liking for the business of making children," she wrote.

A wit at the court, Comte de Tonnerre, noted: "Monsieur is the biggest fool of a woman and Madame the biggest fool of a man I know."

Byron's last poem was to a Greek boy of fifteen. The last lines lament:

> And yet thou lovst me not.
> And never wilt. Love dwells not in our will.
> Nor can I blame thee, though it be my lot
> To strongly, wrongly, vainly love thee still.

John Maynard Keynes, whose economic theories changed the face of the world, was a homosexual. So too was Lytton Strachey, who was the first to write "psychohistories" (which were praised by Freud). These two men, members of the so-called Bloomsbury group, and strongly attracted to each other, were also rivals for the affections of other young men. In at least two instances, Keynes "stole" Strachey's lovers, causing him intense agony.

Still, their friendship survived these crises.

There were other complicated and shifting relationships among the members of this small but ultimately powerful group. Leon Edel, in his splendid biography of the group, *Bloomsbury,* writes: "They were connected by love, a linked chain. Leonard Woolf had originally loved Vanessa's beauty at a distance and Virginia's mind as well as her beauty. Clive had loved and married Vanessa and had wooed Virginia. Vanessa had loved Roger and then Duncan. Duncan had

David Low, *Lord John Maynard Keynes.* "Like Pericles, he gave his name to an age."

been loved by Lytton and then by Maynard and had in turn loved both Keynes and Vanessa. Lytton and Virginia had had that curious love that springs up between a homosexual and a woman because they are comfortable with one another in a nonsexual way. Bloomsbury had broken barriers and had discovered for itself the nature of androgyny; above all, it had understood the relationship between love and sex, where the Victorians had tried to bury sex as if it didn't exist. They had shown that sex could be freed of its Victorian guilt and shame, and that private lives need not interfere with public lives."

A very tempestuous affair ended when Paul Verlaine shot and wounded Arthur Rimbaud, for which he spent two years in jail. Rimbaud, a highly gifted poet of nineteen, never wrote another poem. Verlaine, out of jail, went from one degradation to another and died under the most abysmal circumstances.

Late in the nineteenth century, England passed a law making

even privately performed sex between two males a criminal offense.

The first one convicted under this law was the eminent playwright Oscar Wilde. His persecutor was the Marquess of Queensbury (he codified the rules of boxing), who was incensed that Wilde was having an affair with his son.

The government brought evidence that Wilde entertained several lower-class young men in his apartment. He denied everything, brilliantly fencing with the stolid prosecutor and often evoking admiring laughter from the audience by his witticisms. But he went one step too far: When he was asked whether he kissed one of those young men, he replied, "Oh dear, no, he was a peculiarly plain boy."

That did it!

"Is that why you didn't kiss him?" the prosecutor asked pleasantly.

From there on, Wilde and everyone else knew he was finished.

Convicted, he spent two years in jail. Then he left England and died four years later in Paris, a broken man.

In 1955 the British repealed the law that sent Wilde to jail.

To have known love, how bitter a thing it is.   —OSCAR WILDE

Yet each man kills the thing he loves,
    By each let this be heard,
Some do it with a bitter look,
    Some with a flattering word,
The coward does it with a kiss,
    The brave man with a sword!

—OSCAR WILDE, *Ballad of Reading Gaol*

Some women who listed both sexes among their lovers were Mlle. Georges, the mistress of Napoleon, as well as of his conqueror Wellington; George Sand, lover of Chopin, de Musset, Mérimée and so on; the great Eleonora Duse, lover of many men, chief among whom was the flamboyant Gabriele D'Annunzio; and Colette, who wrote to one woman lover, "My husband kisses your hands, I the rest."

Big Bill Tilden. Love/forty.

William ("Big Bill") Tilden, Jr., an acknowledged tennis genius and the first American to win the finals at Wimbledon, was twice convicted of having homosexual relations. Despite the friendship of presidents, of Charles Chaplin, Greta Garbo, and other notable men and women, he served nine months of one term, and for parole violation was sentenced again, this time to a road gang.

He died an outcast, lonely, broke and abandoned, in 1953.

But in 1981, when another great Wimbledon champion publicly acknowledged a homosexual affair, she received wide support from the public and from most of the companies whose products she helped to advertise.

The times, they are achanging . . .

Most incidents of homosexual and bisexual conduct among legislators and staff members in Washington, D.C., are hushed up in deference to public opinion, but hardly cause any comment in official circles.

A senator who was caught in a male bordello suffered the consequence of public exposure, as did the arrest of one of LBJ's most important staffers in a public comfort station; but these incidents are relatively rare and are dismissed, as someone said, as "just another case of AC-DC in D.C."

Incest
(Also see Family)

Wishing to marry his sister, Cambyses, king of Persia, called together his royal judges and asked them whether there was any law permitting him to do so. In due time they came before him and solemnly declared that while they could find no such law, there was a provision that the king of Persia could lawfully do *anything he wished to do.*

Comforted by this judgment, the king decided to marry *both* of his sisters.

Later on he killed both of these sister/wives.

Brother and sister marriage was compulsory among the pharaohs of Egypt. It was given a religious basis, but it also kept the kingdom in the family.

Such marriages were commonplace among the nobility as well—and even among some of the peasants (to keep the property in the family).

When the Lord destroyed Sodom and Gomorrah, only Lot and his daughters escaped (his wife having turned into a pillar of salt for looking back).

They took refuge in a cave, where Lot's daughters plied him with wine. When he was drunk they "coupled" with him. Their excuse was that since all the men of the cities had been killed, they would never have husbands or children, nor would Lot's line be continued.

Lucas van Leyden, *Lot and His Daughters.* Because their mother was now a pillar of salt, there was none to say them nay.

Incestuous marriages were known to exist among the Ptolemies of the Greco-Macedonian Dynasty. Cleopatra was married briefly to her brother.

When Caligula's sister (with whom he had an incestuous affair) died, he ordered a complete suspension of state affairs. It became a capital crime to laugh or to go to the baths.

The trial and execution of Beatrice Cenci in Rome in 1599 was later the basis for Shelley's poetic drama *The Cenci.* She murdered her father for committing incest with her and then shutting her away.

It was generally accepted that Napoleon had incestuous relations with his sexually precocious sister Pauline. His brother Lucien was accused of similarly sinning with their sister Caroline while she was married to General Murat. Said Napoleon: "The laws of morality are not applicable to me."

In England, in 1940, a man who was accused of the crime of incest with his daughter was allowed to introduce evidence that although she was born during his marriage with the girl's mother, he did not believe that she was *his* daughter.

New York Times, August 2, 1979: A brother and sister, separated as infants, found each other twenty years later, fell in love and lived with each other. Since they did not conceal their relationship they were arrested, tried and convicted for the crime of incest.

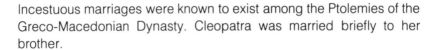

Jealousy

Because of jealousy, the writer George Sand and poet Alfred de Musset quarreled and separated. Sometime later she sent him a lock of her hair. He sent her a lock of his own. She sent him a flower from her garden.

They flew into each other's arms.

(Heinrich Heine said of George Sand's lover: "Musset, ah Musset—there's a young man with a promising past.")

Ludwig van Beethoven's *Kreutzer Sonata* for violin and piano was originally dedicated to the violinist Bridgetower, who was partly black. But when they played the sonata together, the young woman they were both attracted to showed a marked preference for the handsome violinist, causing Beethoven to change the dedication. Kreutzer, the beneficiary of Beethoven's jealousy, never even got to play the sonata.

Beethoven loved the beautiful Countess Giulietta Guicciardi and dedicated his *Moonlight Sonata* to her. She was attracted to him but married the vacuous Count Gallenberg. Many years later, as he tells the story, they met again and Giulietta's effort to resume the affair was coldly rejected by him.

Czar Peter killed his wife, Catherine's, lover and had the head pickled and placed prominently near her bed. But she never flinched and never confessed, and when the Czar died she became ruler of Russia as Catherine I.

V. G. Bernard, *Peter I.*

Claude Monet, *Nana*. Zola's wife's jealousy yielded to her maternal instinct.

Emile Zola *(Nana, Germinal)* at the age of fifty took a young mistress, by whom he had two children. His wife often threatened to kill him if he did not quit the affair.

Childless herself, she was relentless in her hatred for Zola's other family. She never left him, though she constantly threatened to.

But when Zola died, she applied to the court to legitimize his two children, thus enabling them to inherit his name and, when she died, his estate as well.

James "Big Jim" Fisk, one of the most notorious of the robber barons of the post–Civil War period (involved in railroad swindles, an attempt to corner the gold market and so forth), was murdered by Edward Stokes, jealous over the affections of the glamorous courtesan, Josie Mansfield.

(As Fisk had purchased a colonelship in the Ninth Regiment of New York, his great funeral turned out the Ninth's full complement of uniformed men, including a band of two hundred pieces.)

Gabriele D'Annunzio was possibly the shortest poet/lover/politician/ military hero on record. Jealous of his many affairs, Eleonora Duse, the great actress, said, "His life is like an inn; everybody goes through it."

Regarding his various affairs, Napoleon said that Josephine was needlessly jealous. "She is always afraid I will fall in love. Love is not for me, for it is a passion which casts all the rest of the universe aside. . . . Surely I am not the type of man to deliver myself over to such exclusivity of objective. So why should she distress herself over these innocuous diversions of mine?"

But when he thought that Josephine did not regard *him* as an "exclusive objective," he did indeed "distress" himself, writing to her: "What do you do all day, madam? What is the affair so important as to leave you no time to write to your devoted lover? Of what sort can be that marvelous being, that new lover who absorbs every moment, tyrannizes over your days, and prevents your giving any attention to your husband? Josephine, take care! Some fine night, the doors will be broken open, and there I'll be!"

Josephine played Napoleon false, but no more so than he her.

Sam Houston abandoned his bride and a chance to become president and returned to the wigwam of his adopted father, the chief of the Cherokee Indians.

Sam Houston was slated by Andrew Jackson to succeed him as president. A great war hero, noble of bearing and speech, reelected as governor of Tennessee, just married to a beautiful girl, his future was assured; nothing was lacking.

Except that shortly after his marriage he suddenly resigned as governor of Tennessee and *as citizen of the United States,* left home and traveled a thousand miles to join the Cherokee Indians, with whom he had lived for two years as a boy (renamed the Raven by his adopted father, the Indian chief).

There, as gossip raged, he "married" the Indian girl whom he had known in the old days.

The best guess about the reason for his extraordinary conduct appears to be that the girl he married was in love with her childhood sweetheart but that her parents had pressured her into the alliance with Houston, hoping she would become the First Lady of the nation. Further, that on their wedding night she was revolted by his advances, causing him to believe that she was unfaithful to him.

Years later Houston returned to Washington in full Indian regalia as ambassador of the Cherokee Nation, seeking to rectify America's injustice against them.

Jackson convinced Houston that his real destiny lay with his own people. But he remained a friend of the Indians for the rest of his life.

Sam Houston finally did become president—of the Republic of Texas.

In 1859 Congressman Dan Sickles killed Philip Barton Key, the son of the author of "The Star-Spangled Banner," and in his defense pleaded temporary insanity.

Key had made love to the congressman's young Italian-American wife and jealousy had unhinged Sickles's mind, he claimed. This was the first such defense ever offered in an American court. The jury acquitted Sickles, thus starting a trend in criminal trials that continues to this day.

Among the first to take advantage of the "Dan Sickles defense" (really the American equivalent of the French "crime of passion" defense) was Harry K. Thaw, who shot and killed Stanford White, who was having an affair with the beautiful chorus girl, Evelyn Nesbit. John Barrymore was one of Nesbit's lovers, but was successful in keeping his name out of the sensational case.

John Keats to Fanny Brawne: "The air I breathe in a room empty of you is unhealthy. You can be happy without me. Any party, anything to fill up the day has been enough. Who have you smiled with? All this may seem savage in me. Do not write me if you have done anything which it would have pained me to have seen. . . . If you still behave in dancing rooms and other societies as I have seen you I do not want to live. If you have done so I wish the coming night to be my last."

The last sentence of his last letter:

"I wish I was either in your arms, full of faith, or that a thunderbolt would strike me."

Fanny Brawne was attractive and spirited and only eighteen years of age. And so she liked to dance and to flirt mildly, though it is generally felt that her devotion to Keats was genuine.

But the fact that he was dying far away from home without ever having possessed her and that others were enjoying her good nature and her animal spirits drove him to utter despair.

Peggy Schultz, the very wealthy American mining heiress, married the son of Prince von Hohenloe-Ingolfingen. But then she fell in love with Morton Downey, the Irish tenor, which caused her jealous husband, in the very best tradition of the Polish nobility, to shoot himself. But not fatally, which caused his mother-in-law to comment that it was strange that so good a marksman should miss his heart at such short range.

"We despise a man who is jealous of his wife because it shows that he does not love her in the right way, since it is not, properly speaking, she whom he loves, but just the good he conceives as consisting in having sole possession of her, and he would not fear to lose this good did he not judge himself to be unworthy of it."   —RENÉ DESCARTES

Thomas Hart Benton, *Ballad of the Jealous Lover of Lone Green Valley.*

Kings, Queens, Emperors, Empresses

Love according to the twelve Caesars was nothing less than a continuous, mounting, ruthless and cruel exercise of unrestrained passion over powerless subjects.

On his way up the political ladder Julius married and divorced a number of women, besides having affairs with many others. In addition, he was accused of sexually accommodating certain monarchs for political reasons. They said of him that he was "every woman's husband and every man's wife."

If Caesar had a genuine love for any woman it was Servilia, mother of Brutus. Query: In assassinating Caesar, was Brutus motivated Oedipally, politically or both?

When Antony learned that Augustus was opposed to his relations with Cleopatra he wrote to him: "Are you faithful to Livia? My congratulations if when this letter arrives you have not been in bed with Tertullia or Terentella or Rufilla or Salvia or all of them. *Does it really matter with whom you perform the sexual act?"*

It was said of Augustus' mother that while she was asleep in the Temple of Apollo a serpent glided upon her and entered her. Nine months later Augustus was born, suggesting a divine paternity. Later in life Augustus dreamed that the sun rose from between his mother's thighs.

Tiberius built a special house on the Isle of Capri where he had bevies of girls and boys perform the grossest acts to stimulate his waning passions. He had thousands tortured and killed, including his adopted grandsons, their wives and children. A law forbidding virgins from being slain was evaded by having the executioners rape them before killing them and then throwing them down "the stairs of mourning."

After his first wives were divorced for scandalous conduct, Claudius married Messalina, possibly the most depraved of all empresses; but

Julius Caesar.

Claudius forgot that his wife, Messalina, was executed by his own decree only the day before.

Caligula. He raped his sister, among others.

no more so than Claudius, whose far-flung sadistic activities horrified all of Rome.

When she publicly and bigamously married a lover, Claudius had Messalina executed. Notoriously forgetful, he asked her attendants, the night after, why Messalina was late for the banquet.

Caligula (Gaius Caesar), the most monstrous of monster Caesars, ravished all three of his sisters.

He sent a messenger to Greece to bring back the wife of the consul general there, used her once or twice and then ordered her never to have sex *with anyone* for the rest of her life.

He would invite whole groups of highborn women to a banquet and, with their husbands looking on, would have them parade in front of him, judge them, select one of them, retire for a while with her, return and give a public account of her sexual performance.

At the age of twenty-nine he was assassinated. Among the participants was the captain of the guard to whom he had often extended his middle finger, wagged it obscenely and made him kiss it.

Otho helped Nero to cover up the murder of his mother and is said to have had sexual relations with him.

Peter Paul Rubens, *Tiberius and Agrippina.*

When a prophet promised Vitellius a long and secure reign if he outlived his mother, he had her starved to death.

Licentious, cruel, greedy, he was a true son of his father, from whom he inherited these qualities. (To curry favor with Messalina, the notorious empress, his father had begged her to grant him the privilege of removing her shoe, which he then would nurse inside his gown and occasionally take it out and publicly kiss it.)

Every afternoon Vespasian would go to bed for a nap, each time taking with him another woman.

When told that he was dying he joked, "Dear me, I must be turning into a god." (The reference being to the custom of deifying the Caesars after their deaths.)

Titus kept a whole troop of eunuchs for his pleasure.

Nero arranged to have his mother, Agrippina, assassinated for conspiring to take power, or so it was charged. When the assassin appeared, she tore open her dress. "Strike here!" she cried. "Strike here at the womb that bore Nero!"

He murdered his first wife, Octavia, his brother Britannicus, his aunt Domitia, and kicked to death the pregnant Poppaea, his second wife.

About to be assassinated, he killed himself, crying, "Jupiter! What an artist is lost to the world! What an artist!"

Unlike other Roman emperors, who preferred young boys as lovers, Galba's preference was for "mature and sturdy men." He enjoyed his reign for a scant seven months before he was murdered and decapitated.

Domitian rivaled Caligula in the extent of his debaucheries and cruelties. He would invite young men to bed with him and have them executed directly afterward. Professing indignation at the immorality of various Vestal Virgins, he had them executed. He ordered the chief Vestal Virgin buried alive and her lovers clubbed to death.

It is almost exactly a millennium from the reign of the first numbered Louis of France to the last one.

Whether we consider Louis I, who was called "the Pious," or the Louis surnamed "the Blind," or the one called "the Quarreler," or "the Fat," or "Saint," or the "Sun King"; whether they were strong rulers or weak; whether they were "normal" or not; no matter how they differed, they all led troubled family lives and complex love lives.

For example: Louis I's sisters led such immoral lives that he banished them (hence, the "Pious"). His wife openly installed her lover at court and his sons rose in armed rebellion against him. One of his sons was called Charles the Bald, who is not to be confused with Charles the Simple or with Charles the Fat, who should not be mistaken for Louis VI, the Fat, whose father's wife tried to poison him and whose son, Louis VII, declared war against Henry II for marrying his ex-wife, Eleanor [even though it was Louis who had had the marriage annulled].

And so it went for 1,008 years, with one Louis after another, until there were no more.

Louis XV was king at five, engaged to be married at seven.

Louis XV became king at five (like his great grandfather Louis XIV) and when he was told two years later that he was engaged to be married to his cousin, the Spanish princess, aged two, he cried silently all day long.

But Louis married the daughter of the king of Poland instead, and according to those in close attendance to the happy couple on their wedding night, he gave proof of his love for his husky wife "not less than seven times."

After producing ten children in eleven years, the queen lost her conjugal fervor, became deeply religious and refused the king on days celebrating the major saints. As time went on, the queen kept upgrading more and more saints until the king was forced into dalliance with a number of unsaintly young women of the court.

Frederick the Great, the renowned warrior-king of Prussia, was known to his generation as effeminate. He made sure to be seen with enticing young women—ballet dancers, generally—in an effort to counter the gossip about him.

His father had been brutal toward him because of his reluctance to ride, to shoot, to play military games.

The tragedy of his life was the death of his bosom friend, with whom he ran away at eighteen, and for which his friend was executed as a traitor. Frederick was transferred to a jail cell from which he could view the execution. When he cried out in agony, his friend looked toward him and said, "Death is sweet for so lovable a friend." A moment later he was decapitated. Frederick fell in a deep faint and was sick for a long time.

No other attachments—not even for his mother—equaled that which he felt for that young man.

Effeminate or not, Frederick overcame whatever revulsion he'd had over soldiering and became the most feared warlord in Europe, establishing a system and mentality that made World Wars I and II a reality.

To the amusement and/or horror of all Europe, Maria Louisa, queen of Spain, got her complaisant husband to agree to appoint a twenty-five-year-old guardsman prime minister. The only qualification of Manuel de Godoy for the post was his ability to satisfy the queen's physical needs, which no combination of dukes, generals, diplomats and such had been able to do satisfactorily.

The real ruler of Spain, the queen would retire to her rooms after attending to matters of state, and sit there patiently waiting for Godoy.

He seldom failed her.

Marguerite de Valois, wife of Henry IV of France, enjoyed a huge number of lovers, who, however, died violent deaths because of her. She was said to have cherished their memories in a somewhat novel manner: She wore an immense hoop-petticoat with little pockets all around it, and in each pocket was the embalmed heart of one of the lovers.

Each new woman was brought by cab to the Tuileries, undressed in an anteroom, taken nude into a room where the equally nude Emperor Napoleon III awaited her and was instructed by Bacciochi, the emperor's factotum, "You may kiss His Majesty anywhere except on his face."

Theodora was born in an outhouse of the amphitheater at Constantinople, her father being the attendant of the bear pits there. A prostitute from her earliest years, she rose to become the wife of the Emperor Justinian. She very soon became the acknowledged power of the empire.

When Justinian entered the women's quarters after her death in 548 he found hidden in an inner room a heretic ex-patriarch of the Eastern Church whom Theodora had kept concealed for twelve years.

According to Herodotus, King Candaules of Lydia wished to prove to his chief adviser, one Gyges, that his queen's body matched the beauty of her face. He positioned Gyges in the royal bedroom so that he could watch without being seen. Or so they thought. Actually, she became aware of his presence, but did not let on.

The next day she summoned the reluctant voyeur and gave him a choice: either kill the king and marry her or be killed himself. He chose the former option. She positioned him in the same spot from which he had viewed her nakedness. When the king was asleep, she signaled him to kill her husband with her jeweled dagger.

Jacob Jordaens, *Candaules Shows His Wife to His Favorite.* The king paid with his life for exhibiting his wife. Her boudoir then became the murderer's *chambre expiatoire.*

In due time, she married her husband's murderer and had him made king—an event, Herodotus says, which was "celebrated in a poem written in iambic trimeter verse."

Catherine I, the widow of Czar Peter the Great, had been an illiterate peasant who had borne Peter five children before he married her. When he died (after having tortured and executed his son), she ruled Russia as Catherine I.

Peter's daughter, Elizabeth, ruled Russia without ever marrying. Among her army of lovers were a waiter, a coachman, soldiers, diplomats et al. Her chief lover was the master of the hunt, who became known as the Emperor of the Night.

While still in her teens, Elizabeth had an affair with a lowly sergeant. When it was discovered, he was sent to Siberia *minus his tongue.* This did not stop other tongues from wagging, "Like father, like daughter."

Catherine the Great was married to Peter's grandson at sixteen. Though compelled by Elizabeth to sleep together, they had no sex for eight years. In the early years of their marriage he played alternately with dolls and toy soldiers.

One night, when the husband acted as a husband, it was cause for national celebration. But the child born to Catherine was believed by many to have been the result of her liaison with the Gentleman of the Bedchamber, whose father had been one of the Empress Elizabeth's lovers.

When Elizabeth died, Catherine's husband became ruler, but he died after six months. She then proceeded to rule Russia for thirty-two years.

Of all her lovers, the most favored was Potëmkin, to whom she addressed burning love letters. Among the terms of endearment to him: "My golden pheasant . . . my peacock . . . dearest pigeon . . . wolf-bird . . . lion of the jungle . . . my beauty . . . my marble beauty . . . my darling like no king on earth."

Catherine II (The Great) referred to her favorite lover as: "my golden pheasant . . . my wolfbird . . . my peacock."

When Empress Maria Theresa's husband, Francis, died, she wrote: "My husband lived 56 years, 8 months, 10 days. Months—680. Weeks 2,958½, Days 40,778, Hours 496,992. Our union lasted 255,744 hours."

She was a strong ruler, the only woman to preside over the Hapsburg Empire in 650 years. Despite her affection for her husband, she never allowed him an important voice in the council meetings. On those rare occasions when he differed with her, she would dismiss him from the meetings.

But it was well known that she never ejected him from her bed, as is attested to by the sixteen children she bore him.

The turbulent love lives of these extraordinary women were in nice accord with the blood and thunder nature of the times:

Mary Tudor ("Bloody Mary"), Elizabeth, and Mary Stuart, Queen of Scots, pursued their rival claims to England's throne ruthlessly, brilliantly and with matchless courage.

They were ruthless with one another as well: Elizabeth, imprisoned by her half sister, Mary Tudor, was in danger of her life and keenly aware of it, while she in turn, having succeeded Mary, not only imprisoned the other Mary, but finally consigned her to the executioner's ax. Nor was there much doubt that Mary was conspiring to deprive Elizabeth I of her throne *and* her life.

When Mary Tudor, a devout Catholic, came to the throne she married the man who would become Philip II, the powerful king of Spain, for she felt that unless she produced a Catholic heir her mother's religion was doomed in England. She died in bitterness, having experienced the ignominy of two celebrated but false pregnancies and the agony of knowing that Philip had been playing her false with other women.

When Elizabeth succeeded her, she was immediately approached for her hand—if not for her heart—by that same Philip, he contending, quite accurately, that he had counseled his wife, Mary, against having her executed. But the Virgin Queen kept him (and other royal suitors) dangling while she gave her heart—if not her body—to various favorites. It was a parlous thing to be Elizabeth's favorite: She sent Walter Raleigh to the Tower on the flimsiest basis, and the Earl of Essex to his death for more substantial reasons. Her

Dying, Elizabeth I (the Virgin Queen) kept her finger in her mouth, regressing to infancy—when she was a child her father had ordered her mother beheaded.

longtime favorite, the Earl of Leicester, hoping to marry her, rid himself of his wife—by murder, it was rumored—but was not rewarded as he had hoped. (Of Philip II she once said that he had tried fifteen times to have her murdered. "How that man must love me," she said with a smile.)

Whether she died a virgin—and if so whether it was because of some physical malformation or for some complex psychological reasons—has never been settled satisfactorily. But when she died, it was with finger in mouth, a pathetic reminder that in infancy she had been deprived of a mother's love by the murderous decree of her own father.

The execution of Mary, Queen of Scots. She married the man who murdered her husband.

The beautiful Mary, Queen of Scots, like the Empress Catherine, had a love affair that needed hushing up. But where Catherine's lover was "merely" deprived of his tongue, Mary's was deprived of his life by her brother—*at her request.* Bloodletting was never far removed thereafter from her affairs of the heart. When her lover, Bothwell, murdered her husband, Lord Darnley, it was suspected by many that Mary was privy to the plot. And when shortly thereafter she married Bothwell, the suspicions appear to have been verified.

Even during her long imprisonment she bewitched one vulnerable man after another into engaging in plans to overthrow Elizabeth.

And here again the ubiquitous Philip II made his appearance as a possible partner in those schemes.

She died dressed all in red, including long red gloves, forgiving the executioner and comforting her weeping friends.

According to the custom, the executioner held her head up by its hair for the spectators to see, but it slipped from his grasp because Mary had been using a wig to cover her gray hair—a final indignity.

(When Philip lay dying, he couldn't understand why his reign had not been more successful—for nobody could deny that he had been an extremely devout church member. He finally came to the conclusion that he hadn't burned enough heretics.)

Law

In Babylonia, a husband could give his wife to a creditor as security for his debts.

In Bourbon France, a gulled husband had the legal right to have his wife consigned to a convent.

On the Isle of Man, a man caught welshing on a promise to marry had one of two options: the ring or the rope. In colonial America the man, as punishment, could be whipped, branded, fined and/or compelled to marry the victim.

American courts from 1633 on allowed lawsuits for breach of promise to marry. In 1661, John Sutton won fifteen pounds when Mary Russel became engaged to another. Richard Silvester collected twenty pounds for his daughter when John Palmer failed to marry her as promised.

Because it is felt that these lawsuits have been used to blackmail victims with the threat of bad publicity, many states (twenty-one at last count) have recently abolished them.

In the remaining states, very few such actions are now being brought because, it is thought, of improving opportunities for women.

But there are suits to recover gifts or money given in contemplation of marriage.

In Pennsylvania, where a defendant pleaded that the woman had seduced *him,* the court held that "it is but the old cowardly excuse set up by the first man: 'the woman gave me of the tree and I did eat.' It did not save the first defendant from the penalty, and cannot, under the law, save this one." *Seibert* v. *Pettit,* 200 Pa. 58

In the sixteenth century, children who married without parental consent were disinherited. Later, a more Draconian law declared such marriages tantamount to rape.

New York Times, Teheran, Iran, July 3, 1980: On July 2, 1980, four Iranians convicted of sexual offenses were buried up to their chests and stoned to death, with the presiding judge casting the first stone. It took the condemned prisoners—two men and two women—fifteen minutes to die.

The women were convicted of prostitution, one of the men of homosexuality, the other of rape.

One Appius Claudius, a patrician, was instrumental in getting a law passed in Rome declaring marriages between patricians and plebeians invalid. Then he fell in love with a plebeian girl. Unable to marry her, he wanted to make her his mistress. The father, an army officer, objecting, stabbed the girl, Virginia, to death.

(Two thousand years later, the police chief of Birmingham, Alabama—"Bull" Connor—also fell afoul of a new law he himself had sponsored, making it a crime for two people who were not married to each other to have sexual intercourse. The first man arrested under this law was Connor himself. His defense was that the law was unconstitutional. He never did serve time.)

In some states in America it is a serious crime—even for man and wife—to have sexual intercourse with each other in an "unnatural" way—whatever that might be.

In 1978, a judge in Madison, Wisconsin, acquitted a defendant of rape charges on the ground that because the girl wore very tight pants, the young man acted "in a wholly natural way."

The decision so enraged the citizens that they conducted a successful recall campaign against the judge.

A woman may be convicted of rape. One woman was convicted in New York State because she assisted her husband in his criminal assault.

In May 1980, in a highly publicized case, a young woman charged that she was raped during a wild weekend party by a guest who was assisted by some of the women. Such an allegation, if proved, could result in a conviction for the crime of rape against those women.

Franklin Roosevelt courting Eleanor. In time past their marriage would have been illegal.

Before 1215, an English man and woman who were descended from a common great-great-great-great-ancestor could not legally marry. Some of the most celebrated marriages in history would not have taken place if this provision were in effect. (Eleanor and Franklin Roosevelt were second cousins.) Sometimes a man who wished release from marriage would "suddenly" come upon evidence that he and his wife were related. The marriage would then be annulled.

In Blackstone's *Commentaries,* which governed the common law of England, a husband and wife are one person in law. The very being or legal existence of the woman is suspended during the marriage and incorporated into that of the husband, under whose wing, protection and cover she performs everything.

Hence, she had no standing in court; only the husband had. For example, she could not go to court to complain of being beaten by him. Only he could sue. Therefore, he would be suing himself. No such case has ever been reported.

These laws were taken over by the American colonies (except for Connecticut and Louisiana) but were later modified.

Nature has given woman so much power over man that the law cannot afford to give her more.   —SAMUEL JOHNSON

In 1968, a man claimed that he was held captive by some women who compelled him to submit to certain sexual practices. They were arrested, tried and convicted.

September 1980 news item:

HE LOVED NOT WISELY—AND NOT TOO WELL

Arab, the bull born on Saint Valentine's Day, was fated to die for love. At the age of four, the prize Holstein fell victim to his amatory inexperience and damaged his most vital asset when he was sent to service twenty-nine heifers in Wales. Veterinarians counseled total abstinence while Arab recuperated. But a few months later, several seductive heifers from a neighboring farm strayed into Arab's pasture and tempted him beyond endurance. After that night of passion, Arab was through as a stud. He wound up as sausages and soup—and the subject of one of England's most celebrated court cases of the year.

Arab's owner, John Lloyd, blamed ninety-six-year-old Sarah Ann Wright, owner of the femmes fatales, for his bull's injury. He sued for $352,000, charging that her heifers had ruined Arab's potentially lucrative career. The judge, Sir Raymond Phillips, heard much solemn testimony about Arab's damaged organ and ruled that the bull had handicapped himself beyond repair the first time around. He awarded Lloyd just $347.24, and quoted a rustic nineteenth-century poem as an epitaph for Arab:

> Pity him, this fallen chief
> All his splendor, all his strength,
> All his beauty's breadth and length,
> Dwindled down with shame and grief,
> Half the bull he was before,
> Bones and leather, nothing more.

Manners and Morals

Confucius was so strict in matters sexual that he thought it was immoral for the coats of a man and a woman to hang from the same peg.

"When we come to look at the ethics of love at the time of the Renaissance, we are struck by a remarkable contrast. The novelists and comic poets give us to understand that love consists only of sensual enjoyment and that to win this, all means, tragic or comic, are not only permitted but are interesting in proportion to their audacity and unscrupulousness. But if we turn to the best of the lyric poets and writers of dialogues, we find in them a deep and spiritual passion of the noblest kind. . . . And both modes of feeling were then genuine and *could coexist in the same individual.*   —JACOB BURKHARDT

"He who has not lived before 1789," sighed Talleyrand, "cannot know how charming life could be."

One of those charms, for the lords of the manor, was "the right of the first night" *(le droit du seigneur),* which permitted him to deflower the brides of his serfs, if he should feel so disposed.

Pierre Beaumarchais's play *The Marriage of Figaro* (upon which Mozart's opera was based) dealt with this situation. Its performance caused his arrest and was believed by many, including Napoleon, to have helped to feed the fires of the French Revolution.

(Recently, a famous newspaper publisher publicly declared that her husband had approved of her liaison with President Franklin D. Roosevelt. "He considered it a case of *droit du seigneur,*" she wrote with charming inaccuracy.)

At Versailles, a group of dukes, marquises and princes formed a society whose one and only rule was that none of them would have sex with a woman. Their secret amulet was a small golden cross showing a man with his foot on a recumbent woman.

(Three centuries later, a statue titled *Civic Virtue* was placed at City Hall, in New York City, showing a huge muscular young man of noble bearing, with his foot on the body of a naked young woman. She looks up at him imploringly, or adoringly, or possibly both. The statue, subsequently removed because of protests, disappeared for some years and then reappeared in Queens County, where, presumably, a more favorable artistic climate prevails.)

Madame, Louis XIV's sister-in-law, writes to her sister about life at Versailles: "Some [men] can love only men. Others love men and women. Others only children of ten or eleven years of age. . . . Some debauch themselves with anything that comes along—cows and men alike. I know a man who boasts of having got through everything, toads included."

The Marquis de Montespan, unlike most husbands of the favorites of Bourbon kings, resented the loss of his wife to Louis XIV and showed it by driving up to Versailles in a coach draped in black, with a pair of stag's antlers wobbling about on its roof.

Etiquette in some German courts required one of the maids of honor to sleep in the same bedroom as the married sovereigns.

If the queen was not vigilant, this sometimes resulted in some unexpected somnambulism by her husband.

Both men and women were in awe of her beauty, but Pauline Bonaparte was in awe of no one, not even her brother, Napoleon, who, in due time, she listed among her innumerable lovers. Even in that most licentious time she was the scandal of the empire. Often, like Messalina before her, unable to find satisfaction with the generals, diplomats or servants of her household, she went out into the streets, more or less disguised, to pick up the first passerby who seemed attractive to her.

After her first husband, General Leclerc, died in Santo Domingo (she had an affair on the ship when returning with his casket), Napoleon married her off to the immensely wealthy Prince Borghese. When someone said to her that the prince was ungainly, she replied, "Two million a year is always handsome." But when another wished her a happy honeymoon, she laughed. "Honeymoon! With that ass? Is it likely?"

Pauline Bonaparte had an affair on the ship returning with her husband's body.

Casanova's commitment to love was total, and the total of his commitments was awesome.

Casanova had 116 mistresses by name and hundreds more un-named. Or so he said. He distributed his favors in the most democratic manner—noblewomen, chambermaids, whoever—in all kinds of places and positions.

Among them was a beautiful nun who had a semi-impotent lover who wished to watch Casanova's performance through a keyhole. Casanova and the nun obliged him—with what effect upon the voyeur's potency we are left to wonder.

Once, when he wanted to marry a girl, it developed that he had once been her mother's lover, and furthermore, that the girl was his own child. He therefore resumed his affair with the mother instead.

A few years later, the daughter married an impotent, infertile marquis who was anxious to have an heir. Casanova obliged him *and* his daughter by impregnating her. Or so he said.

The Princess Matilda Bonaparte tells of a time when an old and decrepit king said she should have married him: "You must be joking; why you can't even blow your own nose," she said. The king: "Well, what of it? I should have rung the bell and my valet would have turned me over."

When Napoleon saw someone in a crowd who appealed to him, he would send for her, and neither she nor her mother was ever known to have objected. In one case the mother came along and waited all night in an anteroom while Napoleon dallied with her daughter.

D. H. Lawrence, author of *Lady Chatterley's Lover, Sons and Lovers,* etc., urged Frieda von Richthofen, cousin of the Red Baron (the famous German WWI air ace), to leave her husband and children and elope with him.

Her affair and subsequent marriage to him outraged her family, not only because of the immorality involved, but because Lawrence was "lowborn," a miner's son.

In the forties and fifties, a practice among "swinging" couples arose that scandalized America and came to be known as "Boston Key Parties."

A number of couples would have a party at which the men would place the keys to their cars in a hat, and then, without looking, each man would pull a key from it. He would then pair off for the night with the wife of the owner of those car keys.

From an interview with college girls: "My chief reason for yielding is that boys are so insistent and I have no good argument against it."

Another: "If I ever find a man who amuses, interests and stimulates me, I shall be as monogamous as a garden club president, but until then I shall go on, with no self-respect, lapping up as many free Scotch-and-sodas as possible and when there's no mutual ground for conversation—making love."

The publication of *The Kinsey Report* outraged many and astonished most Americans in the 1940s. Particularly, such items as: half of the women questioned admitted to sexual intercourse before marriage (the figure is much higher today); 40 percent of married men had been unfaithful to their wives; 37 percent of them had had homosexual relations at some time in their lives.

The current "sexual revolution" is considered by some specialists in the field simply to be an episode in a "permanent revolution" that started at the dawn of history. Despite differences in form and content from one area or period to another, the effort, conscious and unconscious, has been to free one's self to engage in whatever kinds of sexual activity one has the urge for, regardless of what that society may believe to be right or wrong.

Marriage

The facial resemblance between husband and wife who have lived together for many years is undeniable, and is perhaps the result of the conjunction of various biological and psychological factors. Married life is a continual compromise, resulting in the mutual adjustment of the two partners. This ultimate adjustment has, of course, left traces in the facial expressions and physiognomy of both partners. There is, furthermore, the biological speculation that with old age women become more masculine and men more feminine in their facial expression.   —THEODOR REIK

In the *Conquest of Gaul* (written in 55 B.C.), Julius Caesar spoke of the tribal customs of ancient Britons: "Wives are shared between groups of ten or twelve men, especially between fathers and sons; but the offspring of these unions are counted as the children of the man with whom a particular woman cohabited first."

(Some say that they exchanged wives once or twice a year, others that they married for only a year and a day. But these facts are in dispute.)

In Greece, in the classical period, the wife was supposed to have one ideal: not to be talked about, favorably or otherwise. She did not even go to the market.

If the husband entertained friends, it was in the part of the house reserved for men, and he received without the presence of his wife, as is done still today in Moslem countries.

But the Roman wife was always admitted to banquets and spectacles and she received in company with her husband.

Erotic Arrentine pottery. Plutarch advised wives never to disdain the caresses of their husbands, but also not to provoke them either.

A young Lacedaemonian woman, being asked by an acquaintance whether she had yet embraced her husband, made answer: No, but that he had embraced *her.* And after this manner, in my opinion, it behooves an honest woman to behave herself toward her husband, never to shun nor to disdain the caresses and dalliances of his amorous inclination when he himself begins, but never herself to offer the first provocation, for that savors of impudent harlotry. —PLUTARCH

The wife of Prime Minister Gladstone, a true Victorian lady, wrote of her wedding night: "I simply lay back and thought of England." Or, depending on the source of the anecdote, it was Queen Victoria, or Mrs. Stanley Baldwin, or yet another Englishwoman heroically honoring her marriage vows.

William Cory to Mary Coleridge: "My father was ten years older than my mother. He let her fall out of his arms when she was a baby. Picking her up he said, 'Never mind, darling! I'll marry you some day.' And he kept his word."

Pierre and Marie Curie.

This is how Eve Curie summarized the life of her parents: "She was a woman; she belonged to an oppressed nation; she was poor; she was beautiful. A powerful vocation summoned her from her motherland, Poland, to study in Paris, where she lived through years of poverty and solitude. There she met a man whose genius was akin to hers. She married him; their happiness was unique. By the most desperate and avid effort they discovered a magic element, radium. This discovery not only gave birth to a new science and a new philosophy, it provided mankind with the means of treating a dreadful disease."

When his wife died, Mark Twain wrote in his diary: "She has been dead two hours. It is impossible. She was my life and she is gone; she was my riches, and I am a pauper. She was the most beautiful spirit, and the highest and noblest I have known. And now she is dead."

Though Sir Thomas More preferred the younger of two sisters, he married the elder out of a sense of pity.

Unlike the biblical Jacob, who was first tricked into marrying Leah before he could marry Rachel, her younger sister.

And unlike Mozart, who married Constanze, the younger Weber daughter, because her older sister wouldn't have him. ("He's too short," Aloysia said, which was also one of the reasons that Josephine didn't react favorably toward Napoleon for quite some time.)

Phidias made the statue of Venus at Ellis with one foot upon the shell of a tortoise to signify two great duties of a virtuous woman: to keep at home and be silent.

George Sand's first marriage, when she was very young and inexperienced, to the "natural son" of a baron of the empire was a miserable experience.

What her first night must have been like may be deduced from a letter she sent many years later to her son when his daughter was about to be married:

> Try to prevent your son-in-law from brutalizing your daughter on the wedding night. . . . There is nothing so frightful as the terror, the suffering and revulsion of poor children, ignorant of the facts of life, who are subject to violation by brutes.

The union of the American "aristocracy," arising primarily from wealth, and the European variety, based upon lineage, assumed epidemic proportions with the burgeoning of the American economy, especially following the Civil War.

Not only have Goulds, Vanderbilts, Astors, Bakers, Mellons et al., from New York, Philadelphia, Boston and Newport made the grade, but so have many less illustrious names from Sacramento, Kalamazoo and Pearl River.

These young women have enhanced both the fiscal and physical fortunes ("beefed up the lines," as one cattle raiser put it), of such storied houses as: the dukedoms of Marlborough, Argyle, Rutland, Windsor, Talleyrand-Perigord, Sermoneta, de Montesquiou-Fezensac, de Zoagli and de Sagan.

They have married such as the Grand Duke Dimitri of Russia; the Earls of Gramard, Dessborough, Dudley and Warwick; Lords Churchill and Plunket; the Marquess de Surian and Vicomte de Rosier.

They have become the Countesses Bismarck, d'Eudeville, Quintanilla, de Cosse-Brissac, Rucellai, de Pourtales, Robilant, Berkeley, de Marigny, Gaetani, Crespi, de Rochambeau, Vitetti, Senni, de Capodelista; the Princesses Hohenlohe, Scherbatow, Lobkowicz, Radziwill, Ilynski, Djordjaze, della Rovere, San Faustino; Marquesses of Waterford, della Stufa de Cuevas; Baronesses Aberconway, Lo Monaco, de Pellenc, d'Erlanger, de Rothschild and Pantz.

During medieval times, the lord of the manor could determine who married whom. If a girl married without leave, her father was fined.

In Basel, in 1411, it was prescribed that every year, before Shrove Tuesday, the bailiff might allot to each boy of marriageable age a mate from among the girls of that town.

In 1300, the theological encyclopedia: "A man may chastise his wife and beat her for her correction . . ."

Even Saint Thomas More, in his celebrated *Utopia* (the perfect society he envisioned), proposed that husbands chastise their wives, and on "holy days the wives [should] fall down prostrated before the feet of their husbands, confessing their offenses."

In a book on chivalry, it was declared that the husband may beat his wife only "reasonably."

Of one thousand letters responding to a questionnaire, 40 percent of the husbands and 20 percent of the wives said that the nature of their sexual relations was the main marital problem.

The music at a wedding reception always reminds me of the music of soldiers going into battle.   —HEINRICH HEINE

If you're afraid of loneliness, do not marry.   —ANTON CHEKHOV

The Duke and Duchess of Windsor. Wallie was not the only Baltimore belle whose marriage a royal establishment frowned upon. Napoleon put an end to the marriage of his brother to the beautiful Betsy Patterson of Baltimore.

Twice divorced Bessie Wallis Warfield of Baltimore, Maryland, married the crown prince of Great Britain, but never became queen because of his abdication.

One hundred thirty years before, another belle of Baltimore, Betsy Patterson, married Napoleon's young brother, Jerome, while he was visiting the United States. Napoleon was furious, commanded Jerome to return, set him up as king of Westphalia and got his marriage annulled.

According to English common law, a man might beat his wife with a rod no thicker than his thumb.

Saint Bernardino of Siena, preaching against women's fashions: "Oh, if I were your husband I would give you such a drubbing with feet and fists that would make you remember for a while!"

The problem men have with their wives arises, according to one learned if excitable divine, because: "She is more wanton than the ape, more venomous than the asp." Which is why she is in need of correction—physical as well as spiritual.

A French guide of duties and usages (1530) contains the cautionary account of the woman who was rash enough to scold her husband in public. "He smote her with his fist down to earth, and then with his fist he struck her in the visage and broke her nose and all her life after she had her nose crooked."
     A word to the wise wife . . .

Battered wives make a scandalous case against our civilization, but since the advent of the women's liberation movement they are striking back in growing numbers. One estimate: two hundred thousand cases of assault upon husbands by hitherto submissive wives; still far less than the assaults *against* them.

There are some good marriages, but no delightful ones.
                                        —FRANÇOIS LA ROUCHEFOUCAULD

One should always be in love; that is the reason one should never marry.   —OSCAR WILDE

It is a mistake for a taciturn, serious-minded woman to marry a jovial man, but not for a serious-minded man to marry a light-headed woman.   —GOETHE

Miscellany

The word for *love*—or other terms indicating affection or tenderness—did not exist in primitive tribes.

Primitive man was not interested in the sexual response of the female. The removal of his sexual tension was the only important thing. With the individualization and personalization of sexual life, the importance of the response of the female partner increased more and more. (Balzac said that some husbands are like orangutans with a violin.)

There is no word for "bachelor" in the Hebrew language.

In Plato's *Symposium* Aristophanes describes love as the urge of an originally androgynous being to find his split-off half. Love is thus the desire and the pursuit of the whole. Love is the hunger for unity.

Because of widespread concubinage among the priests, a papal legate was sent (1126) to deal with the scandals. But he himself was then caught in bed with a harlot.

Borgia Rodrigo Lanzol, later Pope Alexander VI, engaged in a liaison with Rosa Vannozza dei Cattanei, who gave birth to five children by him. He betrothed his daughter Lucrezia, twelve years old, to a Sforza. The marriage was dissolved because of the groom's impotence. Yet she later gave birth to a child.

The pope then issued two Bulls, in one of which he named himself as father, in the other naming his son Cesare as the daughter's lover.

Lucrezia then married the Duke of Besaglia, the illegitimate son of the king of Naples. But Cesare, still in love with his sister, strangled the duke with his own hands. Again available, Lucrezia married the Duke of Ferrara.

The last married Pope was Adrian II (867–872). There was no specific obligation to celibacy for the first thirty-seven popes.

Marozia ruled Rome early in the tenth century. She had Pope John X, her mother's lover, thrown into prison, where he was murdered, and replaced him with John XI, her son by her lover, Pope Sergius III. Twice widowed, Marozia married the king of Italy, Hugh of Provence. But Alberic, her son by her first marriage, banished Hugh and ended Marozia's power.

"Passionate love is the supreme form of happiness." Stendhal. Marc Chagall, *Lovers (left),* and Hisikawa Haronobu, *The Lovers (below).*

Tapestry, *The Gift of His Heart.*

Stendhal postulated four kinds of love: (1) physical love, (2) love through taste, (3) vanity love, (4) passionate love. (1) is meeting a fresh young peasant maid while hunting in the woods; (2) a higher stage of affinity through the appeal of taste; (3) the French manner of love, for the sake of social pretensions; (4) the highest and strongest form.

Passionate love was the supreme source of happiness. "To love is to feel alive." He combines this with a sense of beauty in music, art and literature.

Leonardo da Vinci re the phallus: "It sometimes has intelligence of its own. It is obstinate . . . it moves without permission, waking or sleeping. . . . Man is wrong in being ashamed to give it a name or exhibit it, seeking constantly to conceal what he ought to adorn and display with ceremony as a ministrant."

The symbol of Priapus, son of Aphrodite and Dionysus, was the phallus. Huge phalli were carried in sacred religious festivals.

Since love provides security, reassurance and releases therapeutic energy, lack of it causes sickness, even death. It may also turn the individual toward various forms of antisocial conduct. Infants in institutions where personal relations—handling, caressing, smiling and so forth—are absent, often sicken and sometimes die.

Senator William Proxmire, a Treasury watchdog of bulldog determination, upon learning of an $84,000 National Science Foundation grant to study the difference between "passionate love" and "compassionate love," declared, "I object to this not only because no one—not even the National Science Foundation—can argue that falling in love is a science. I'm also against it because I don't want an answer."

J. P. Morgan was celebrated for his power, his money, his art collection, his three-hundred-foot yacht, his bulbous red and purple nose and his taste in women.

When he was young he collected the autographs of Episcopalian bishops; it was said that when he grew older he collected the bishops themselves. Among the functions they performed for him, from time to time, was to accompany him on voyages aboard his yacht along with one or more of the young beauties he fancied. Precisely what theological duties the church dignitaries engaged in on these trips remains a mystery.

In any case, Morgan bestowed generous settlements upon an extensive list of the female guests who lightened his hours aboard *Corsairs I, II* and *III* and contributed handsomely to the church as well.

Because of an understandable exercise of self-censorship, the Masterpiece Theater's production of the life of Lillie Langtry did *not* contain the following dialogue:

PRINCE OF WALES: I've spent enough on you to buy a battleship.

LILLIE LANGTRY: You've spent enough *in* me to float one.

In many primitive societies the phallus was thought to have a separate life, mind and movement. It was a man's other self, his alter ego. It was an appendage directed by another being who had to be placated by magic and incantations. By witchcraft too it could be rendered immobile.

Mary Cassatt, *Le Baiser*.

In men the nature of the genital organ is deaf to reason, disobedient and self-willed.   —PLATO

I see another law in my members warring against the law of my mind and bringing me to captivity to the law of sin.   —SAINT PAUL

"Love brings on a giddy response comparable to an amphetamine high. And the crash that follows breakup is much like amphetamine withdrawal."

Dr. Michael R. Leibowitz and his colleague Dr. Donald F. Klein, conducting a scientific study of love at the New York State Psychiatric Institute, report that the reason for the similarity may be that the loving brain pours out its own chemical correlate to amphetamine—phenylethylamine—while the spurned brain stops production of the substance and immediately begins to suffer from its absence. The doctors noted that when a rejected lover turns into a chocolate junky—as often happens—it may be because chocolate is loaded with phenylethylamine, the chemical produced by the brain when in love.

Musicians

Johann Sebastian Bach, whose twenty children were impeccably legitimate, was in the service of Augustus II, elector of Saxony and king of Poland, who had, it was claimed for him, 365 known illegitimate children.

Gioacchino Antonio Rossini, composer of *The Barber of Seville* and *William Tell* (and whose first music teacher played the piano with only two fingers), married a famous courtesan, Olympe Pélissier, and lived happily with her for twenty-one years despite contrary predictions. When he died, she threw herself across his body and cried aloud, "Rossini, I shall always be worthy of you!"

He loved his mother fervently, and some say that this was what motivated him to compose the opera *Semiramide,* about Babylon's queen and her son-lover.

Franz Liszt.

Countess Marie d'Agoult met Liszt, became pregnant by him, abandoned her husband and two children for him, bore three of Liszt's children and then convinced his mother to bring them up.

In a letter to a friend, in which she wrote at length about hats and dresses, she added this postscript:

"I forgot to tell you—I was confined last month in Rome—a boy. I left him there . . . Madame Albert did likewise."

Rejected by the singer Aloysia Weber, Mozart married her sister Constanze. He wrote candidly to his family about her: "She is not ugly, but at the same time far from beautiful. Her whole beauty consists in two small black eyes and a handsome figure. She has no wit, but sound common sense to be able to fulfill her duties as a wife and mother."

Ludwig van Beethoven fell desperately and completely in love with many women, some of whom, however, tended to marry aristocrats. After he died, his letters to "My Immortal Beloved" were discovered. Despite intense investigations by innumerable scholars, the object of these passionate outpourings remains obscure. There are at least six women who could qualify for this description.

Peter Tchaikovsky, thinking that he might overcome his homosexuality, married a determined pursuer, Antonina Milyukova, his student, and spent an agonizing two weeks with her before escaping—with the aid of one of his younger brothers, himself a homosexual.

His abandoned wife went from affair to affair, produced several illegitimate children and died after a lengthy stay in an insane asylum.

In his last year, Tchaikovsky composed his Sixth Symphony (known as the *Symphonie Pathétique),* which Havelock Ellis called "a homosexual tragedy."

The libido of Richard Wagner, the extraordinary opera composer, seemed most intensely aroused by the wives of his friends and patrons.

In fact, his most abiding affair—and subsequent marriage—was with the wife of his close friend, Hans von Bülow (and daughter of another friend, Franz Liszt).

Ellin Mackay's fabulously rich father violently opposed her marriage to Irving Berlin, the composer ("Easter Parade," "I'm Dreaming of a White Christmas"). He took his daughter on a world tour (including an audience with the pope) in order to detach her from Berlin, who was Jewish.

While she was away, Berlin composed "All Alone" and "Always."

When she returned, her father threatened Berlin that he would disinherit Ellin if she married him. To which Berlin retorted that on the day they married he would sign over to her $2 million—half of his fortune.

Despite predictions to the contrary, the marriage was a permanent and happy one.

Philosophers

According to Plato, Sophocles, remarking on the manner in which the physical passions fade with advancing age, concluded that it is "like being set free from service to a band of madmen."

"Mistresses we keep for pleasure, concubines for daily attendance upon our persons, and wives to bear us legitimate children and be our housekeepers."

In none of these relationships does Demosthenes mention love as an element.

When Nero ordered Seneca, Rome's leading philosopher, to commit suicide, he did so by cutting his wrists. Upon his wife's insistence, he cut hers as well.

Expatiating on the superiority of men, Aristotle said that a man's semen contains the principle of the soul, while the female's secretions contribute only to the material of the body.

And so, because the wife is inferior to the husband "she ought to love him more than he her."

Hypatia, the beautiful lecturer in philosophy at the museum in Alexandria (around A.D. 350), attracted men of learning from distant lands.

When a young man declared passionate love for her, she lifted her dress to her waist and said: "This is what you are in love with—not anything beautiful."

René Descartes tells us that he found himself especially attracted by a squint in the female face, and . . . traced it to his boyish fancy for a girl who had a cast in her eye.

The great philosopher and mathematician lost his mother when he was only a year old (she died in childbirth). He loved the surrogate who became his wet nurse and provided for her during his life and in his will.

Like Jean Jacques Rousseau, he made an alliance with a servant girl whom he never married, though he had a child by her. And like Rousseau, he sought his mother in women his whole life long.

Arthur Schopenhauer, the notorious misogynist, quotes Byron approvingly: "Women ought to mind the home. They ought to be well fed and clothed, but should not mix in society. Well educated too in religion, but to read neither poetry nor politics—nothing but piety and cookery—and a little gardening."

Poets

When Dante first saw his beloved Beatrice, both were nine years old— a fact of great significance for him because three is the perfect number, the number of the Trinity. Nine is the square of three—three raised to a still higher power. What was more natural than that Beatrice was a female of superhuman perfection? Dante only saw her a few times and never spoke to her, but she was his pure and perfect love all his life, even though he married and had a number of mistresses.

The meeting of Dante and Beatrice.

Clodia, who came from an ancient patrician family, captivated all of Rome, including the poet Catullus. He claimed that her body exuded a fragrance so intoxicating that "one would like to be all nose," the better to enjoy it. Calling her Lesbia in his love poems, he at first defended her against charges brought by Cicero, including that of murdering her husband. But when she took on lover after lover, including her brother, he turned bitterly against her.

While he wrote his celebrated sonnets about the purity of *his* love for Laura, Petrarch had a mistress by whom he had two illegitimate children.

(The real Laura had eleven children—all by her husband.)

For forty-seven years, Petrarch, influenced by Dante, wrote innumerable sonnets to Laura, his "pure and perfect" love.

> Think you, if Laura had been Petrarch's wife,
> He would have written sonnets all his life?
>
> —BYRON, *Don Juan*

Ironically, one of Marquis de Sade's direct ancestors was Hugue de Sade, husband of Laura, who was the inspiration for Petrarch's delicate poetry. The sadistic de Sade was responsible for two deaths in a brothel by giving the women candy with a dangerous dose of Spanish fly extract—cantharis.)

When John Milton's wife died, he wrote a sonnet beginning, "Methought I saw my late espoused saint . . ."

Lorenzo da Ponte, Mozart's librettist, was a friend of the notorious libertine, Casanova. When da Ponte married, he introduced his wife *as his mistress* in order not to lose caste in his friend's eyes.

(Envious of Casanova's reputation for "gallantry," da Ponte wrote: "I know that extraordinary man as well as anybody ever did and I can assure my readers that love of truth was not the principal excellence of his writings.")

England's great trio of romantic poets all had tragic love lives and all died tragically young in foreign countries—Keats and Shelley in 1821 and Byron in 1824. Despite caste and temperamental differences, they aided one another in many ways.

Shelley was hounded by the authorities for his radicalism, but after his wife, Harriet—whom he left for Mary Godwin—committed suicide, he became a pariah to polite society. When his body was found drowned in the Bay of Spezia, a copy of Keat's poems was in his coat pocket.

Byron's ostracism, though he was a lord of the realm, was even more total than Shelley's, because one of his many affairs was with his half-sister, Augusta. He died at Missilingeh, Greece, while attempting to unite various guerrilla groups into an effective fighting force against the Turks. His last poem was to a Greek boy of fifteen.

Son of a stable keeper, John Keats was dead at twenty-six, never having possessed the one girl he ever loved, Fanny Brawne. He died in a house on the Spanish steps of Rome, comforting his grieving friend Joseph Severn with his last breath, "Severn, lift me up for I am dying. I shall die easy. Don't be afraid."

From his last letter to Fanny: "I cannot exist without you. You have absorbed me. I have a sensation of dissolving."

When Goethe had grown old, he was visited by the young and beautiful Bettina Brentano. She had found love letters from him to her mother and on impulse decided to repeat her mother's triumph. She dressed herself in some of her mother's finery and came to Goethe's home unannounced. When he looked up, she stood framed in the doorway in a pose such as she had seen in pictures of her mother.

The "sage of Weimar" was stunned by this apparition of his old flame; but not so stunned that he failed to embrace her when she threw her arms about him. Indeed, he aided her to unbutton her dress.

Charles Baudelaire considered his mistress to be depraved and stupid. "Stupidity is often the adornment of beauty; it is what gives a woman's eyes that mournful limpidity of dark pools, that oily tranquillity of tropical seas. Stupidity is often the preservative of beauty."

GEORGE GORDON, LORD BYRON.

PERCY BYSSHE SHELLEY.

JOHN KEATS.

Passionate about beauty, love and freedom, all three poets died tragically young and in exile.

When Heine's illness was in its terminal phase, his wife pleaded with him not to die, crying, "Last week my parrot died, and now you—I couldn't stand it."

Bedeviled by poverty, alcoholism and the hostility of the critics, Edgar Allan Poe secretly married Virginia Clemm, his thirteen-year-old cousin. They lived through twelve unrelievedly harsh years together, until Virginia died, Poe following her a year later.

The following is the last stanza of *Annabel Lee,* expressing Poe's anguish over his young wife's death:

> For the moon never beams, without bringing me dreams.
> Of the beautiful Annabel Lee;
> And the stars never rise, but I feel the bright eyes
> Of the beautiful Annabel Lee:
> And so, all the night-tide, I lie down by the side
> Of my darling—my darling—my life and my bride,
> In the sepulchre there by the sea—
> In her tomb by the sounding sea.

Emily Dickinson, one of America's very best poets, had one tragically aborted love affair. Thereafter she lived reclusively, writing more than one thousand poems, many of them on scraps of paper or on backs of envelopes. Only seven of them appeared in print in her lifetime.

> So we must keep apart,
> You there, I here,
> With just the door ajar
> That oceans are,
> And prayer,
> And that pale sustenance
> Despair!

John Donne wrote poetry to his wife until the day she died (after her twelfth child).

We love with our minds and senses. The heart counts for very little in love.
—HEINRICH HEINE

ELIZABETH BARRETT BROWNING.   ROBERT BROWNING.

Elizabeth Barrett fell deeply in love with Robert Browning, but her father violently opposed the romance. (He was, in fact, opposed to any of his children marrying.) It took considerable courage for her to flee her father's house and run off with Browning. The following is the most famous of her *Sonnets from the Portuguese,* expressing her passion for her lover:

> How do I love thee? Let me count the ways.
> I love thee to the depth and breadth and height
> My soul can reach, when feeling out of sight
> For the ends of Being and ideal Grace.
> I love thee to the level of everyday's
> Most quiet need, by sun and candlelight.
> I love thee freely, as men strive for right;
> I love thee purely, as they turn from praise.
> I love thee with the passion put to use
> In my old griefs, and with my childhood's faith.
> I love thee with a love I seemed to lose
> With my lost saints—I love thee with the breath,
> Smiles, tears, of all my life!—and, if God choose,
> I shall but love thee better after death.

What is irritating about love is that it is a crime that requires an accomplice.   —BAUDELAIRE

Politicians

Aaron Burr, former vice-president of the United States, married the infamous Mme. Betsy Jumel when he was seventy-seven. She was the daughter of a prostitute and herself had a daughter when she was a prostitute (the name of the midwife was Mrs. Freelove Ballon). Enormously rich and eccentric, she married Burr forty years after she first met him, when, as a beautiful prostitute, she served him and many others. Some even say that the duel between him and Hamilton was really over her.

Betsy had tricked Jumel, a very wealthy Frenchman, into marrying her, and consequently she met Bonaparte, Talleyrand and others in French society. When he died, she was courted for her money by Burr, now despised, bankrupt, alcoholic. She finally yielded, but he wasted so much of her money and, though old, had so many extramarital affairs that she eventually threw out this man who almost was president of the United States when she was a prostitute. He died a few months later.

When Benjamin Franklin was the American emissary to France, he became a great favorite among the women of the country's outstanding salons, despite being over seventy years of age.

Among his adventures was one with Mme. Brillon, a chess enthusiast. She engaged him one enchanting day in a game of chess while she was in her bath.

The next day he wrote her, apologizing for having "detained her" so long in her bath and asking her forgiveness for his "indiscretion." Exactly what indiscretion he committed is not spelled out.

Queen's gambit accepted? Declined?

The American minister to France, Gouverneur Morris, despite having only one leg (the other was lost, according to some, while escaping from a wrathful husband), was famous for his love affairs.

One of them was with the wife of the Comte de Flahaut, who was also mistress to Talleyrand, by whom she had a son. She told Morris

The duel between Aaron Burr and Alexander Hamilton. At seventy-seven, despised, bankrupt, alcoholic, Burr married the woman whose services he had paid for when he was thirty-five.

Benjamin Franklin in Paris. He told a woman he was courting that he dreamt he went to heaven and saw their departed spouses embracing. "Come, madame," he wrote, "let us avenge ourselves!"

that she knew a count who was the reputed lover of a marquise, his sister, and that the mistress of another count was his daughter.

The wife of Benjamin Disraeli, Queen Victoria's unlikely prime minister, drew up a balance sheet comparing her qualities and tendencies with her husband's:

HE	SHE
Very calm	Very effervescent
Manners grave and almost sad	Gay and happy-looking when speaking
Never irritable	Very irritable
Bad-humoured	Good-humoured
Warm in love, but cold in friendship	Cold in love, but warm in friendship
Very patient	No patience
Very studious	Very idle
Often says what he does not think	Never says anything she does not think
It is impossible to find out who he likes or dislikes from his manner	Her manner is quite different, and to those she likes she shows her feelings
No vanity	Much vanity
Conceited	No conceit
No self-love	Much self-love
He is seldom amused	Everything amuses her
He is a genius	She is a dunce
He is to be depended on to a certain degree	She is not to be depended on
His whole soul is devoted to politics and ambition	She has no ambition and hates politics

---

Peggy Eaton was a barmaid who caused a cabinet to fall.

When her husband committed suicide, she married Senator Eaton. Scandal!

But President Andrew Jackson liked Eaton and was fond of Peggy, who had often served him food and drink at the inn that many politicians favored. In defiance of the scandalmongers, he appointed Eaton Secretary of War. (He felt that Peggy was being victimized by

Peggy Eaton, the barmaid who caused the nation's cabinet to fall.

the same kind of gossip that had caused his wife, Rachel, such misery.)

The women of fashion and power boycotted Peggy's socials. Jackson, enraged, ordered his cabinet members to attend Peggy's next function with their wives. When the women rebelled, he fired his whole cabinet. A national and international sensation! Jackson was called "King Andrew," "Sharp Knife" and the like, and all the old scandals were dusted off and aired for the delectation of the public.

Because Martin Van Buren was loyal to Peggy, Jackson supported him for the presidency. "Petticoat politics," the opposition jeered.

But Van Buren was elected.

The extraordinary sisters Victoria Woodhull and Tennessee Claflin, daughters of a stableman, leaving local lovers and husbands behind, stormed New York and took it.

Preaching the doctrine of free love and practicing spiritualism and "animal magnetism," they magnetized Vanderbilt, Gould and Fisk, who set them up in the banking and brokerage business, the first women to own and run such sacred institutions.

Victoria Woodhull, running for the presidency, said that marriage was worse than prostitution because a prostitute could turn the customer away.

Victoria ran for president in 1872, the first woman to do so (with Frederick Douglass as running mate). Program: freedom for women and blacks and free love. She maintained that marriage was worse than prostitution because a prostitute can turn the customer away, but the wife cannot deny her husband.

The country was scandalized.

Sex without pleasure, she said, is a crime. Men must learn that women enjoy sex as much as they do, and therefore find it abhorrent when there is only obligation and no enjoyment.

Anthony Comstock, of the Society for the Suppression of Vice, had the sisters arrested for immoral activities.

The sisters retreated to England where they married very rich and eminently respectable gentlemen. As philanthropic widows, the sisters aided the poor and distressed in both America and England for the remainder of their very long lives.

Huey Long, U.S. senator, who was one of the great demagogues of the thirties and aspired to the presidency, was assassinated in New Orleans for reasons not ever fully understood.

Once, it was reported, when he was a passenger aboard a train, he attempted a sexual assault on a young woman. When reproached by his own friends, he said, "Well you gotta try, don't you?"

Almost all the wives of politicos operating out of Washington, D.C., testify to the difficulties of maintaining a life of reasonable domestic felicity. The main reasons are the stress of responsibilities, the problems of staying in office, of social standing and, perhaps most of all, the sexual temptations to which their men are subjected.

Divorce, alcoholism and general unhappiness have been the rule among a high percentage of these families. Only lately have these wives felt free to speak of their difficulties, including mental and physical breakdowns.

The "companions" of their husbands are generally young, unattached women who work in the offices and are attracted to those whom they consider the power elite.

The frequent and long campaigns away from home for reelection are among the occasions for sexual promiscuity, although they seldom result in anything more than ad hoc affairs.

Political "groupies," not unlike those who gather around rock stars (except in the sense of style), are a constant source of temptation, which is why many wives go along on the campaign trail with their husbands.

The scandals among the high and the lower echelons go unreported by the press, unless some incident becomes a police matter, such as the affair of the "Tidal Basin," where the chairman of the Ways and Means Committee was costar of the comedy-drama along with a stripper known as the "Argentine Firecracker."

Potency

Martin Luther caused an uproar by counseling women whose husbands were impotent to contract a secret bigamous marriage. He said a woman should address her husband thus: "Look, my dear husband, you are unable to fulfill your conjugal duty to me. . . . In the sight of God there is no real marriage between us. Grant me the privilege of contracting a secret marriage with your brother or closest relative and you retain the title of husband . . . being betrayed voluntarily by me."

Under the Code of Hammurabi (about 1700 B.C.), a childless wife was permitted to choose a servant to give to her husband for childbearing purposes. If the mating was successful, the servant could not be sold. She was free and her child was legitimate.

In Rome, it was acceptable practice for wives to be lent or given to a friend. Cato, the younger, gave his wife, Marcia, to Hortensius, who wanted to have children by her.

Augustus' wife, Livia, was given to him by Claudius. Later she became empress.

The Chevalier de la Tour Landry wrote about a group of men and women who called themselves Galois and Galoises. The husband of a Galoisie, receiving a fellow Galois under his roof, was bound, under penalty of dishonoring himself, to give up house and wife to his guest for the duration of his stay.

In Sparta, under Lycurgus, a man who was advanced in years and had a young wife could recommend to her some young man of virtue and health by whom to have a child, which would then be accounted the husband's. Lycurgus felt that the laws of other nations in this regard were absurd; that they were more solicitous of the breeding of their dogs and horses; that they paid money to secure the services of quality breeders but shut their wives away and often mated with them though infirm or even diseased, resulting in the debasement of the race.

Delilah, bribed by the Philistines, seduced Samson into revealing that the secret of his fantastic strength was his hair. Whereupon she cut off his crowning glory while he slept and thus rendered him helpless.

Most moderns believe that "hair" was a euphemism for genitalia. However that may be, the ancients did believe in the magical powers of hair in both men and women. Julius Caesar, Tiberius and other rulers were very sensitive about their baldness, even as men are to this very day. One U.S. senator, Proxmire of Wisconsin, went through the painful process of hair transplants and claims to feel much better about himself as a result.

Emperor Augustus, in his efforts to obtain an heir, divorced two wives. His third wife catered to him by procuring young girls for him, the belief being that only virgins could restore his potency. It didn't work for Augustus any more than it did for King David:

King David was coming to the end of his days. In an effort to revive him, his wife, Bath-sheba, brought a beautiful young girl, Abishag, to his bed, but "he knew her not," reports the Old Testament (meaning that he was unable to perform). Upon his death his son Solomon inherited Abishag, as was the custom. When his brother asked that she be given to him, Solomon took this to be a challenge for the crown and had his brother slain.

In Italy, when a wife charged her husband with impotence, he had the legal right, up to the sixteenth century, to disprove the allegation before witnesses—either in a brothel or at home.

Vincenzo Gonzaga, duke of Mantua, so proved himself, before a group of dignitaries of the Church (but we are not told where and with whom).

Samson and Delilah. Was it his hair she sheared?

Napoleon's Farewell to Josephine. "I am not bound by the laws of morality."

Napoleon divorced Josephine and married Marie Louise of Austria because fathering a son by young Countess Walewska had convinced him that Josephine's failure to produce an heir was not his fault but hers.

(Countess Walewska, Josephine and a Mme. Gazzani, also once one of the Napoleon's mistresses, came together after the divorce and were friendly.)

The daughter of the Count Palatine of the Rhine said that her father died from exhaustion, due to trying—vainly—to satisfy the needs of his robust young Swiss mistress.

The Duc and Duchesse de Chartes were so fond of making love that when dining out they generally asked for the use of their hostess's bed during the course of the meal. They generally returned in time for dessert.

Anna Gould left her husband, Comte Boni di Castellani, when he had squandered five million Gould dollars. She next married his cousin, the Duc de Talleyrand. There was some speculation about the connubial capacity of both of these titled gentlemen.

After William Harvey's discovery of the circulation of the blood, attempts were made to rejuvenate old men by blood transfusions from virile young men. The few reported improvements resulting from this technique were believed by specialists to be purely psychological.

A theory later developed that hot-blooded husbands and frigid wives—or vice versa—could benefit from mutual blood transfusions, equalizing their temperaments and, presumably improving their lives. Whether any couples benefited from this bloody procedure seems, at the least, highly questionable.

Sheep's blood was injected into the veins of impotent men. But while they did not bleat after the injection—as had been feared by some—neither did their sexual performance show improvement.

Later, monkey's glands were transplanted, with similar results.

Transfusions of sheep's blood did not make the impotent bleat, but it did not make tigers of them either.

Frazier, the sensational geriatric folk hero.

Some years ago, one of the great safari parks in the United States imported a number of young virile lions to mate with a group of nine lionesses in residence there.

But the lustful young males were summarily rejected by every one of the lionesses, leaving them as well as the safari managers totally frustrated.

It was at this juncture that fate and Frazier took over. Frazier was an ancient, near twenty-year-old has-been of a lion, with shrunken shanks, loose-hanging skin, almost toothless, a mane in name only— all in all a "King of the Jungle" fit for nothing but abdication.

Or so everyone thought.

He had been sent to the safari park by a Mexican circus that had no place anymore for so woebegone an animal, and had solicited a final resting place for it from the park managers.

The morning after Frazier arrived, the keeper of the big cats was met with an astonishing sight: Frazier lolling on his back, all four feet in the air, the picture of a contented if exhausted animal, surrounded by a circle of admiring females.

When the keeper brought their food later, they fought briefly among themselves for the honor of bringing the king his meat. And then waited until he had eaten before falling to themselves.

Frazier reigned alone among the lionesses for four love-filled years, resulting in the births of thirty-six cubs.

When word of this geriatric miracle reached the public, Frazier became an instant folk hero, celebrated in song and story, the ultimate accolade being the wide sale of T-shirts embellished with the portrait of "King Frazier."

The safari park received a large number of discreet inquiries concerning Frazier's diet.

Several Nobel Prize winners have agreed to contribute to a "sperm bank," designed to produce "superior" progeny. Their sperm is or will be available upon the request of "properly qualified" women—according to one report.

One commentator: "They should have to prove their solvency like any other bank." Another: "It may result in millions of children who can discuss the 'black holes in space' and nothing else; or Heisenberg's 'principle of uncertainty' and be unable with any certainty to know right from left or love from hate."

Presidents and Presidents' Wives

George Washington was fond—overly fond some said—of Sally Fairfax, his good friend's wife. Late in life, he wrote of the "happiest moments of life" that he had spent with her. When the furnishings of the Fairfax Mansion were sold at auction, he bought the pillow from her bedroom.

There were a few who professed to believe that Alexander Hamilton was Washington's "natural" son, but the majority believed with John Adams that he was the illegitimate son of a Scottish peddler.

John Adams declared, "My children can rest assured that no illegitimate brother or sister exists or ever existed." He was believed because he was married happily to Abigail for half a century. But two months before the Declaration of Independence was signed, she wrote him that the unlimited power of husbands must be changed or "we are determined to foment a rebellion and will not hold ourselves bound by any laws in which we have no voice or representation."

Adams replied, "As to your extraordinary code of laws, I cannot but laugh! We have been told that our struggle has loosened the bonds everywhere—children and apprentices, schools and colleges, Indians and Negroes grow insolent. But your letter was the first intimation that another tribe, more numerous and powerful than all the rest, were grown discontented. . . . Depend on it, we know better than to repeal our masculine systems."

According to some, a persuasive case has been made for the proposition that Thomas Jefferson had children by a beautiful young slave on his plantation after his wife died.

The story was given wide circulation by the press during his lifetime. He neither admitted nor denied the charge. Some historians feel that there is insufficient evidence to support the allegations.

When James Buchanan was a young man of twenty-nine, his fiancée, Annie Coleman, committed suicide by taking a large dose of laudanum. This tragedy was used by his political enemies against him, the rumor being that she had reacted to his unfaithful conduct.

This gossip had been circulated by her brothers to dissuade her from marrying Buchanan, for they believed him to be an "upstart" and "not good enough" for their sister.

Believing her brothers, Annie fell into a deep depression, resulting finally in her suicide.

Buchanan, deeply affected by the tragedy, remained a bachelor all his life, the only American president to do so.

Abraham Lincoln's tragic romance with Ann Rutledge is well known, but his relationship with Mary Owen is not.

Out of his loneliness he found himself engaged somehow to this "agreeable and intelligent" woman even though her size made her "a fair match for Falstaff," as he wrote to a confidante after it was all over. He regretted his initial impulse to commit himself to her but was determined to go through with it as a matter of honor. "If you've made a bad bargain, hug it all the tighter."

Whether she detected his true state of mind or changed her mind for some other undisclosed reason, she declared that she would not marry him after all.

To his surprise he found that now that she had rejected him, "I began to suspect that I was really a little in love with her." He added that he doubted that he would ever marry because, "I can never be satisfied with anyone who could be blockhead enough to have me."

And then he met Mary Todd . . .

Andrew Jackson killed Charles Dickinson in a duel for insulting his wife, Rachel. They had married in the belief that her divorce from her first husband, Lewis Robards, was legal when it was not. When the facts were disclosed, she was accused of bigamy and adultery. It was over these charges that Jackson engaged in the duel with Dickinson. He received the first shot—an almost mortal wound, his own shot then proving fatal to Dickinson.

A cartoon of Andrew Jackson that appeared after he fired his cabinet.

Rutherford B. Hayes's sister, Fanny, and Hayes and Mrs. Hayes.

Rutherford B. Hayes was under the domination of his sister, who even accompanied him on his honeymoon. Even after she married, she said that it was her brother who was "the love object" of her dreams.

When she died, Hayes said to his wife, "Now you must be what my sister was to me."

John Quincy Adams was accused by Andrew Jackson's allies, during the 1824 election campaign, of "giving" an American girl to the czar when he was ambassador to Russia.

Warren G. Harding had a child by his young mistress, Nan Britton, when he was senator from Ohio, and continued his relationship with her for some time after his election as president, including assignations in the White House itself. He contributed to her support right up to the time of his death, while still in office.

Because of the refusal of Harding's family to recognize the child as his, Nan wrote a book that caused a sensation.

Upon Harding's sudden death, rumors arose to the effect that Harding's wife poisoned him—either because of jealousy over his affair with Nan Britton and/or to save him from impending scandal and impeachment due to the infamous oil lease thievery by his closest friends and associates (known as the "Teapot Dome Scandal").

This theory was given further credence because of the widow's refusal to allow an autopsy to be performed. In addition, the Surgeon General who was Harding's physician died not long afterward, just as suddenly as Harding had, with Mrs. Harding present at the same White Oaks Farm. Some believed that she disposed of him because "he knew too much," but most authorities summarily dismissed these rumors.

In the presidential election of 1884, the Republicans were certain that their candidate was a shoo-in when they came up with the information that a Buffalo widow, Maria Halpin, had a child who, she said, was fathered by Grover Cleveland, the Democratic candidate.

Cries of "libertine" and "moral leper" shook the country, and all other issues were for a time forgotten. With glee and the certainty of victory, the Republicans chanted: "Ma! Ma! where's my pa?" The Democrats answered: "Gone to the White House, ha, ha, ha."

But Cleveland behaved well. Claiming the "pardonable frailty" of youth, he took full responsibility and revealed that he had been taking care of the child.

Cleveland was elected.

Another voice for Cleveland.

Grover Cleveland never denied that he fathered Maria Halpin's child.

President and Mrs. Wilson.

About eight months after his wife died, Woodrow Wilson fell in love with and married Edith Galt, a widow.

Sigmund Freud and William Bullitt, collaborating on a book about Wilson, declared that he suffered from an unresolved Oedipus complex and that both his wives were mother substitutes.

When Wilson suffered a paralytic stroke, his wife, for all intents and purposes, became chief executive of the United States. His friends denied it, but it remained the opinion of Freud, Bullitt and many commentators.

Harry S Truman is one of the few presidents of whom no romantic scandal has ever been heard. The only family involvement to have caused comment was his public attack against a critic of his beloved daughter, Margaret's, singing voice. He publicly called the critic "an SOB."

(A critic, Petronius, who sent Emperor Nero a message that he was "the worst singer in history," cut his veins and died right after sending the message, for he knew that Nero would order his execution for this treasonable comment. Apparently the critic felt that his own life was a small price to pay for the satisfaction of telling the aesthetic truth.)

Fortunately, Margaret's critic did not feel the obligation or necessity of following Petronius' example.

In 1918, when Eleanor Roosevelt discovered the affair between FDR and Lucy Mercer, her social secretary, "The bottom dropped out of my particular world," she wrote.

Later, when FDR began a relationship with his secretary ("Missy" LeHand), Eleanor made the acquaintance of Lorena Hickok, a newspaper reporter. Through the years that followed, and unknown to the world, her feeling for "Hick" grew in depth and in intensity until it became an affair with significant emotional and physical overtones, as expressed in the hundreds of passionate letters that she sent to "Hick."

The publication of these letters in 1980 created a sensation; many people refused to believe in their authenticity, others interpreted the passionate phrases as "innocent" expressions of affection, while still others, believing in the astonishing revelations, were disenchanted or thought it unwise to "sully the name" of one of the great First Ladies in American history. However, many were glad that she had a friend to make up for the emotional deprivations in her life.

Eleanor Roosevelt in photo taken by F.D.R. during their honeymoon in Venice.

Dwight and Mamie Eisenhower shortly after their marriage. Would he really have divorced Mamie?

Kay Summersby, one of Dwight D. Eisenhower's drivers in Europe during World War II, wrote a manuscript in which she claimed to have had an affair with him and that he had wanted to marry her.

Near the end of his life, President Truman revealed that "Ike" had indeed sent a letter to General Marshall declaring his intention to divorce Mamie and marry Kay; that Marshall brought the letter to him and that he had it burned, declaring that if Ike went through with the divorce he would deprive him of his rank.

According to Kay Summersby, Eisenhower was more effective as a military commander than as a lover. She died of cancer before completing the book.

Despite being married to a glamorous wife, John F. Kennedy is known to have had a number of affairs, before and during his presidency.

As time goes on, the number of those who claim to have had sexual relations with him has assumed epidemic proportions. One woman, the mistress of a notorious gangster (since murdered), claims to have had dozens of assignations with him right in the White House.

Lyndon B. Johnson boasted so openly and to so many of his sexual adventures that some skeptics have doubted the validity of his claims.

His wife, Lady Bird, said, "A politician ought to be born a foundling and remain a bachelor."

Not a single rumor has ever been circulated—either by friends or foes—that Richard M. Nixon was ever even tempted to engage in extramarital adventures.

However, "Bebe" Rebozo, Nixon's close friend, gave an example of Nixon's ribald sense of humor (on a Walter Cronkite program). He told how they played a joke on another Nixon confidant, Robert Abplanalp: "We had a couple of these ladies' legs—it looks like real legs, they're skin colored and all; they're blown up. And Abplanalp was going to come over and visit us so we decided to play a trick on him, and we borrowed a wig and a wig stand from a neighbor, put it in bed with the wig hanging over the thing, and the legs sticking out from under the sheet. Bob came in, and when he saw that, he didn't know whether to act like he didn't see it, or leave it or what, but it was a riot."

Three wives of presidents died while their husbands were in office: Letitia Tyler, Caroline Harrison and Ellen Wilson.

Ida McKinley, an epileptic, suffered a seizure during her husband's second inaugural ball.

The death of the son of President Franklin Pierce in a railroad accident caused his wife such overwhelming grief that she wore black for the rest of her life.

Mary Lincoln was accused by some of acting as a Southern spy because her brother and others in her family fought on the Southern side.

Grover Cleveland's widow was the first president's widow to remarry.

Prostitution

The great Greek festivals, though religious in origin, were used as sexual safety valves.

There was no stigma in the use of courtesans, and Athens recognized prostitution in the most practical way by taxing it. There were three orders (the common brothels were marked with a phallic symbol). The man could bargain for whatever period of time he required, including taking the prostitute home with him.

Sacred or temple prostitution in Babylon and elsewhere in near and middle eastern civilizations was under supervision of the religious institutions, the funds going to them. This commerce was thus given religious sanction.

Brought up by Pericles and taught by Socrates, Alcibiades was the favorite of all Athenians. Brilliant, talented and sought after by everyone, he distributed his favors among men and women alike, but he found the greatest sexual satisfaction with the lowest caste of prostitutes.

Solon, the celebrated lawgiver, having established brothels in Athens, drew enough revenue from them to build a temple to Aphrodite.

Cicero defended prostitution because without it men would break up their marriages and live with mistresses.

Prostitution is still defended in this way by some, the prostitutes being called "gardens of virtue," for they keep young men from violating the purity of "decent" young women.

Herewith, an example of this logic:

A woman of fifty, "Tired of Sex," writes to Dear Abby: "On the same page of your column in our local paper, a news item appeared announcing that the court had ordered the closing of four brothels that had been in business in Deadwood, S.D., since 1876.

"This caused an uproar in the little Black Hills tourist town of 2,500. Some citizens wrote letters to the editor, saying, 'There's nothing wrong with prostitution—it keeps the nuts off the streets, and keeps our women and children safe.'

"Well, I think legalized prostitution would sure do a lot for some of us tired wives (me included).

"I've often thought how nice it would be for both of us if, on his way home from work, my husband could stop at a place that was given a four-star rating by the health department. After all, I believe his need is physical, not emotional.

"But I know my husband wouldn't take advantage of it because he'd consider it immoral—darn it!"

Henri Toulouse-Lautrec, *Au Salon de la Rue des Moulins.*

In the fourteenth and fifteenth centuries the hangmen of Munich and other south German towns were appointed as the "chastisers" of prostitutes.

Prostitutes in France in the time of Charles the Bold were required to wear veils, the colors differing in different towns.

The duke of Alba allowed a train of eight hundred mounted prostitutes to follow his army.

In many towns in France the prostitutes had official associations, the head of which was known as the queen.

In fifteenth-century Rome, on Shrove Tuesday, immense throngs of prostitutes and their friends would gather in the Piazza Nuova and sing vulgar songs and otherwise carry on.

In ancient Scottish law—and in German law too—prostitutes were thrown down deep wells.

In London, during George III's reign, girls under ten walked the streets or were sold into brothels.

In some brothels boys and men were for sale, either to women or to men.

When Benjamin Disraeli informed Queen Victoria about a law then being debated regarding the regulation of prostitution, she exclaimed in horror, "Prostitution in London?" Disraeli: "London is one vast whorehouse, madame."

Alexander Hamilton's affair with a prostitute whose husband pimped for her and blackmailed him was disastrous for his career.

There was also a rumor that he was intimate with his wife's sister. She in turn wrote her sister, playfully, it was believed, "If you were as generous as the old Romans, you would lend him to me for a while."

Large corporations hired prostitutes to secure orders for their equipment. They took the contracts to bed with them and when the prospective buyer was at his most dynamic would insist that his signature precede any further dalliance.

Prudery

Lysistrata, the comedy written by Aristophanes (which dealt with the refusal of the women of Athens and Sparta to share their husbands' beds until the dreadful war was brought to an end); aroused the authorities in Pittsburgh, Pennsylvania, twenty-five hundred years later, to demand certain deletions in the text before they would permit it to go through the mails.

In Los Angeles, a warrant for "the arrest of the author, Aristophanes," was issued, but later retracted.

Michelangelo decorated the wall behind the altar of the Sistine Chapel with scenes from the Last Judgment. He painted all the figures,

Aubrey Beardsley, *Lysistrata Haranguing the Athenian Women.*

including the angels, as altogether nude. When he was finished, the Vatican was appalled, but hesitated to protest.

When a new pope came to rule as Pope Paul IV, he ordered the figures to be painted over with loincloths. The job fell to a former student of Michelangelo, Danielle de Volterra (who was thereafter dubbed the "Pants-maker" by his colleagues).

In Victorian times prudery went so far as to cause some people to pull pantaloons over the legs of the grand piano.

Michelangelo painted a version of Leda and the Swan. When the Inquisition went after the picture, it was smuggled out to the Court of Francis I in France. It was safe until the reign of Louis XVI when it was burned.

Michelangelo, *Leda and the Swan.* The Inquisition did not approve of this painting.

Gustav Flaubert was prosecuted for writing *Madame Bovary,* Baudelaire for *Fleurs du Mal,* de Sade for everything.

Dr. William Alcott, a reputable physician, said that the reason women seldom make sexual advances is that it is not natural for them to have sexual feelings.

(In Greek legend the god Zeus and his wife, Hera, argued over whether men or women derived more pleasure from the sexual act. They put the question to Tiresias, who responded that the woman derives nine times as much pleasure as the man does. Hera, infuriated, struck him blind for that answer.)

Prudery in the 1850s: Genteel people ate the "bosom" of chicken, not the breast. . . . One medical professor expressed pride in American women who preferred "to suffer the extremity of danger and pain" rather than be examined vaginally by doctors. "I say it is evidence of a fine morality in our society."

Advice to young women in America in 1845: "Sit not with another in a place that is too narrow. . . . Read not out of the same book. . . . Do not have conversations which are too exciting."

Anthony Comstock, the scourge of sin, sex and scandal (his activities gave rise to the term *Comstockery)* and who as head of the Society for the Suppression of Vice prosecuted authors and publishers for works he considered pornographic, used to confiscate photographs that he claimed violated public morals. He kept thousands of these photos, often showing them to people to prove how sinful they were. He was not known to have destroyed them.

Race

Because Richard M. Johnson, vice-president in Van Buren's administration (1836), openly maintained three black mistresses, Andrew Jackson demanded that he be dropped from the ticket in the next election.

In antebellum South, the visible evidence of the sexual relations between masters and slaves was everywhere—light-skinned slaves. The wives seldom dared complain, but they suffered from the sense of deprivation and rejection. Often they took it out on the female slave, even though they knew that she was generally the husband's unwilling victim (though occasionally a slave girl would consent to the connection because she hoped that the master would protect her and her children).

Mary Chestnut, wife of the senator from South Carolina who became a leader of the Confederacy, wrote with great indignation against the sexual relations between white men and female slaves: "The mulattoes one sees in every family resemble partly the white children. Any lady is ready to tell you who is the father of the mulatto children in everybody's household but her own. My disgust boils over."

One of the great scandals of the 1920s: The eminently social Leonard Kip Rhinelander married Alice Jones, who was black.

(Fifty years later, a secretary of state, Dean Rusk [of Georgia!], at the wedding ceremony of his daughter, gave the bride away to a black man.)

Religion

Herodotus reported that in one temple in Babylon there was a "mysterious room that contained a great bed, richly adorned and beside it a table of gold." Every night the god therein commanded a different woman to come to him.

Two thousand years later Cyrus Spragg built a temple in New Jerusalem, Illinois, an "ecclesiastical palace," which he declared he would enter and remain in "meditation for all eternity."

Only virgins were permitted to enter and serve him with the "necessities" of life.

He declared that one of the virgins—without identifying which one—was destined to give birth to the Messiah. A different virgin came to him every night and was received in total darkness, for no one was permitted to look upon the holy face of "The Invisible Presence."

But his presence, visible and invisible, was suddenly terminated by the jealous suitor of a virgin whose turn it was to serve him.

Muhammad, on the reversal of the "correct" position in sexual intercourse:
"Cursed be he that maketh himself earth and woman heaven."

In medieval times seven years of penance was required from those who, departing from the correct position *(Venus observa)*, engaged in *coitus a tergo* or *more canino* (as dogs.)

Muhammad promised the faithful that they would ascend to heaven, where beautiful black-eyed virgins would be impatiently awaiting their arrival to serve them.

The Koran provides that a husband may beat a rebellious wife.

Muhammadan men could marry women outside the faith; Muhammadan women could not.

In 585, a bishop proposed that women were not only vicious and sinful per se, but that they did not even have a soul.

In view of the controversy over when life begins, it is interesting to note that Saint Thomas Aquinas asserted that a soul entered the body of the male fetus forty days after conception, but that it took eighty days in the case of females.

Saint Augustine established the principle that all copulation was sinful, married or not, because it was the result of lust. He maintained that there would have been no lust if Eve had not seduced Adam into disobeying God. He argued that they could still have followed God's injunction to "multiply," by having sex without lust. How? The genitals would simply be commanded, as other "muscles" are commanded, to respond. He gave, as an example, the fact that people can break wind at will, some even having the ability to do so musically.

Fifteen centuries later such a pyrotechnical performer arose, who gave concerts in Paris in the manner suggested by Augustine.

A Frenchman, Joseph Pujol, became the sensation of Paris by breaking wind professionally. At performances where he was billed as Le Petomane (petomane—an anal emission of gas), he "sang" through his backside, producing a range from tenor to bass. Audiences would be overcome with laughter as Petomane made anal noises like machine-gun fire, or, in his big number, blew out a candle. His act was so popular that he drew gates of two hundred thousand francs while Sarah Bernhardt only managed eight thousand. His poster read:

LE PETOMANE

EVERY NIGHT FROM 8 TO 9

THE ONLY PERFORMER WHO

DOESN'T PAY ROYALTIES TO A COMPOSER.

Confessors' manuals dictated that even marital sex could be performed only in one position—and not on Sundays, Wednesdays and Fridays. Nor on many holidays. And even then only if the object of the act was to create a child.

"Creation, not recreation," as one commentator put it, "should be the object of coitus."

In India, when a man died, the widow, as an act of love and faith, placed herself beside him on the funeral pyre and was burned to death. If the man had several wives, they all joined in the sacrament and immolated themselves. The practice was confined mostly to the upper castes and was based on the belief that a woman had no true life of her own after her husband's death. If she did not go through with this suicide, she was automatically subject to serfhood to her husband's family.

The practice is now outlawed.

An anecdote told by Camille Rousset, the military historian:

After General Sébastiani had repulsed the English attack on Constantinople, the Sultan Selim said to him, "What reward would you like?"

"I would like to see your harem."

The sultan showed him the harem, and then asked, "Is there any woman you liked?"

"Yes," the general said, and indicated which one.

"Very well," the sultan said.

That night, the head of that woman was brought to the general on a platter, together with a message: "As a Moslem, I would not offer you, a Christian, a woman of my faith. But now you can be sure this woman on whom you set your eyes will never belong to any other man."

Anatole France said that Christianity did much for love by presenting it as a sin. Addressing women directly, he said, "To change you into the terrible wonders you are today, to become the causes of sacrifices and crimes, two things were needed: civilization, that gave you the veil, and religion, that awakens scruples within us. With all this done, you become a secret and a sin."

New York Times—July 9, 1980: "Her Conservative Government has 'no plans' to change a controversial 1701 law that would bar Prince Charles from the throne and as head of the Church of England if he should marry a Roman Catholic, Prime Minister Margaret Thatcher told the House of Commons yesterday.

"The ruckus had arisen on the weekend, when the British press erupted with one of its periodic speculations about possible nuptial candidates—particularly Princess Marie-Astrid of Luxembourg, a Roman Catholic—and militant Northern Ireland Protestants demanded assurances that the present prohibition would not be changed."

Prince Charles avoided the problem by marrying Lady Diana Spencer on July 29, 1981.

Saints

"Women are the gates of hell," Saint Origen said, and castrated himself to keep from entering those gates.

Saint Augustine believed that he had finally conquered lust—in the daytime. But Lord, what does one do with the nights? he agonized.

Saint Jerome believed that the study of Hebrew would calm his sex drive. "There is treason in this earthly vessel," he said.

Saint Abraham, in response to Paul's injunction (that it is better not to touch a woman), opted out of a marriage at the very last moment, and found a way to enclose himself within a high tower, leaving an aperture wide enough only to permit food to be passed to him.

Saint Eleazer, on the other hand, went through with the marriage ceremony but lived with his wife without sex.

Some of the devout who married and did have sex tried at all costs not to have any pleasure from it.

Saint Nicholas was saintly even as an unweaned infant, as is proved by the fact that on holy days he is said to have refused his mother's breast.

Saint Simeon Stylites spent thirty years on top of a sixty-foot pillar to avoid succumbing to the temptations of the flesh. Tennyson wrote a poem called "St. Simeon Stylites."

Pope Gregory, who said of women, in his fourth *Dialogue,* that they are, "the gates of hell," praised the priest who took orders and left his wife, despite his love for her. Forty years later, his wife, hearing that he was dying, came to say good-bye. When he saw her he burst out: "Get thee away woman, there is still a little fire left!"

It was the time of Constantine, and tens of thousands retreated to the desert and mortified their flesh. Not alone did they avoid all sexual contact but refrained as well from washing their bodies or their clothes (usually a single ragged garment).

By not eating, washing or even sleeping, they suffered so in the flesh that they were not tempted to sin.

Saint Clement declared that "every woman should blush at the thought that she is a woman."

Saint John Chrysostom convinced his friend not to marry a young woman he fell in love with by saying: "The groundwork of this corporeal beauty is nothing else but phlegm and blood, bile, masticated food."

Saint Paul said: "The head of every man is Christ; and the head of the woman is the man."

Saint Aquinas accepted Aristotle's notion that woman is a defective male, lacking vital force. "The female is a misbegotten male."

Seduction
(Also see Law; Manners and Morals)

In the ancient laws and institutes of Wales, it is provided that if a woman is taken by a man "to bush, or brake or house, and after connection is deserted (that is, seduced and abandoned), she is to receive for her chastity a bull of three winters, having its tail well shaven and greased . . . and then let her take the tail in her hand . . . and if she can hold this bull, let her take it for her face-shame and her chastity; and if not, let her take what grease may adhere to her hands."

Diligent research has failed to uncover any cases in which the aggrieved woman was able to hold on to the greased tail of a three-year-old bull.

In a modern case a man accused of seducing a girl by claiming that he was a prince of the blood was permitted to cite the precedent of the gods in justification:

Jupiter seduced Danaë disguised as a shower of gold, Zeus seduced Leda in the guise of a swan, Europa in the guise of a bull and so forth.

An act of Parliament of 1770 decreed that "all women, of whatever age, rank, profession or degree, whether virgin maid or widow, who shall impose upon, seduce and betray into matrimony any of His Majesty's subjects by means of scents, paints, cosmetics, washes, artificial teeth, false hair, Spanish wool, iron stays, hoops, high-heeled shoes or bolstered hips shall incur the penalty of the law now in force against witchcraft and like misdemeanors, and that the marriage upon conviction shall stand null and void."

Spanish wool?

Often, when a Greek or Roman maiden "suddenly" became pregnant, she would claim to have been ravished by a god. After all, it was well known that Zeus himself often came to earth and sported with human maidens. Everyone knew that.

Augustus considered Ovid's *Art of Love* a licentious work and therefore exiled the author and banned the book.

Ovid suggested that the lustful suitor of another's wife should first seduce the lady's maid, who will then be experienced enough to enjoy provoking the lady's husband to a sexual adventure, which, in turn, will anger the wife so that out of motives of revenge she will dally with the original energizer of the drama.

It was a crime in New York State, punishable by up to two years in jail, "to seduce a female under promise of marriage." In one such case a defendant, convicted and sentenced, appealed on the ground that there was evidence that the woman had previously been seduced by another.

The Court of Appeals reversed the conviction, declaring that a woman cannot be seduced twice. "A case of *seductio ad absurdum,*" someone suggested.

Quoted in the Sunday pictorial of February 6, 1955, is an item from the *Osservatore della Domenica,* a Vatican paper, "Adam was to blame because he should have had more common sense than to get excited over Eve. He should have given her a smart slap in her face when he was aware that he was being gradually seduced."

Warriors

The Romans invited their neighboring states' families to a banquet and then raped and kidnapped the women (the Rape of the Sabine Women). War ensued. The women themselves appeared during the battle, placed themselves between the warring lines and thus brought the war to an end. (Or did they? There is much evidence to the contrary.)

Herodotus insisted that the Amazons, a race of women-warriors, had a marriage law that provided that no girl should wed until she had killed a man in battle. "Sometimes it happens that a woman dies ummarried at an advanced age, having never been able in her whole life to fulfill this condition."

A Lombard princess, Sichelgaita, loved and married the famous Norman warrior, Guiscard, about the year 1180. She fought beside him in all the great battles. When the battles were going badly, it was she who would rally the retreating soldiers and urge them into the fray again.

During the American War for Independence, almost five thousand British women—some wives among them—were brought over from England for the soldiers. In addition, many American women were camp followers of the British—some of them were escaping indentured servants or those whose time had been served.

Jacques Louis David, *The Rape of the Sabine Women.*

General Henry ("Light-Horse Harry") Lee re the British commander, General William Howe: "He shut his eyes, fought his battles, drank his bottle, had his little whore."

He was referring to the general's American mistress, Mrs. Loring, whose whims, many felt, Howe had put above the strategic needs of the war, to the advantage of the Americans.

Her husband was appointed commissary of prisoners for his marital complaisance, enabling him to enrich himself.

Howe was the grandson of George I and a German mistress, the Baroness Kielsmansegge. Howe kept several mistresses occupied, as well as a legal wife.

Philadelphia 1777–78. The British occupied it and fascinated Loyalist women, among them Peggy Shippen. She was attracted to Major André, a handsome and aristocratic major. He designed the Turkish gown Peggy wore for the great ball the British organized, as well as her elaborate coiffeur.

Later, she married Benedict Arnold, the dashing American general who became a traitor. For sixteen thousand dollars and other promises, he delivered the plans of West Point's defense to Major André, who was caught and hung. But Peggy always kept a lock of André's hair in her locket.

In the American Revolution, many wives fought alongside their husbands and sweethearts, the most famous of them being Molly Hayes, known as Molly Pitcher. When her husband fell at Monmouth, she took his place, "sponging, loading and firing the cannon."

A soldier who saw her there wrote that as she reached for a cartridge: "A cannonball from the enemy passed directly between her legs without doing other damage than carrying away all the lower part of her petticoat. She observed that it was lucky it did not pass a little higher, for in that case it might have carried away something else."

Margaret Moncrieffe, daughter of a British officer in New York, was seduced at the age of thirteen. Aaron Burr, notorious for his affairs, was accused.

"I am told," he wrote, "that she gives me the honor of having been the first to take her virginity. But I do not think that would have been possible." Hardly a very definite disclaimer.

Burr suspected her, quite accurately, of being a spy. She painted her messages in code in still lifes of flowers.

Deborah Sampson, disguised as a man, served in the War for Independence. When she fell seriously ill, the doctor who attended her penetrated her disguise but kept her secret. His niece, however, fell violently in love with the handsome soldier, who barely escaped with her anonymity intact—such was the strength of the young lady's passion.

A number of young wives, unwilling to be separated from their husbands, fought alongside of them with admirable courage.

One of them replaced her wounded husband as assistant gunner and suffered "a shredded breast."

The charm and beauty of the most famous of all Southern spies in the American Civil War, Rose ("Wild Rose") O'Neal Greenhow, was one of the reasons for the astonishing defeat of the Union forces in the first Battle of Bull Run.

Young or old, men invariably fell under her spell and yielded up vital secrets concerning the number and disposition of troops and armaments, as well as plans for their use. Bull Run was her first great success.

Even after she was arrested, she continued to receive and dispatch to Jefferson Davis and Generals Jackson and Beauregard vital information. She also continued to give orders to a wide network of spies, including about fifty women.

"Major" Pauline Cushman, whose mother was a great French beauty, was a spy for the North. Her exploits were so outstanding that General Rosecrans himself visited her and made her an honorary "Major of Cavalry." Of all the men who sought her she chose as a lover a physician, who for a time accompanied her as she made her triumphal way across the country with a theatrical company after the war.

But this alliance broke up, as did a subsequent marriage. She lived a colorful, turbulent existence, but ended her career in the direst poverty, exchanging her services as a scrubwoman for a back room in a shabby rooming house. When she died in 1893, the country rediscovered her. She was given a grand funeral parade, with hundreds of Civil War veterans in full uniform as guard of honor.

Her stone reads:

PAULINE CUSHMAN
Federal Spy and Scout
of Cumberland

Belle Boyd, almost as celebrated as Rose Greenhow, fell in love with Samuel Hardinge, a Union naval officer, and he with her. For love of Belle he turned traitor. After they were married he was arrested. Belle, having found refuge in England, wrote a letter to Lincoln threatening to reveal publicly many "atrocious" secrets if her husband was not released. While there is no record that her letter was ever seen by Lincoln himself, one week after the date of her letter the secretary of war issued an order for the immediate release of Belle's husband and his transportation to Liverpool, England.

During World War I, Storyville, in New Orleans, was declared off limits for members of the armed services because of the profusion of houses of prostitution.

This injunction by the secretary of the navy resulted in the spread of jazz to the rest of the nation. The reason was that the earliest jazz musicians were unable to obtain employment other than in those bordellos. So when lack of patrons resulted in the closing of those establishments, the musicians drifted to Kansas City, St. Louis, Chicago, and New York, carrying this new sound to all corners of the nation—and eventually to much of the rest of the world as well.

Karl Marx, the originator of international proletarian revolution, married a young aristocratic woman, Jenny von Westphalen, whose mother was in a direct line of descent from the Earl of Argyle.

Friedrich Engels, his closest friend and collaborator, lived first with Mary Burns, and when she died, with her sister, Elizabeth. He never did marry.

During World War II, the pressure upon young women to have sex with soldiers was intense. It almost seemed unpatriotic not to yield to the young men's (and their own) sexual desires. Often there were unwanted pregnancies, hasty marriages and, later, regrets. When the soldier returned, a couple often found that failing the excitation of the patriotic fever there was no real community of interest between them.

Sometimes the girl would recognize this lack even before the soldier returned and would send him what became known as a "Dear John" letter, saying she no longer loved him, or never really did, and that she was engaged or married to someone else.

On the other hand, soldiers often succeeded with women who were pledged to civilians or were even the wives of nonmilitary men, either because those women felt it the patriotic thing to do or were carried away by the glamour of the uniform.

It caused one commentator to say: "It was ever thus, from the time that Mars gulled the hardworking but gimpy Hephaestus, disporting himself with Venus, his too amiable wife."

During the Vietnam War some soldiers sent semen by air to their wives—to be used for artificial insemination.

Witches

Because women are insatiably sexual and because they are naturally fickle and of low intelligence they are easily led by the devil into becoming witches. And then they copulate with him rather than with their husbands.

So said the Bible of the Inquisition, the *Malleus Maleficarum.* "She is more carnal than a man, as is clear from her many abominations. . . . There is a defect in the first woman because she is made from a bent rib, that is, a rib from the breast, which is bent, as it were, in a contrary direction to a man. And since through this defect she is an imperfect animal, she always deceives . . ."

"What is to be thought of those witches who sometimes collect male organs in great numbers, as many as twenty or thirty together, and put them in birds' nests or shut them up in a box, where they move themselves like living members, and eat oats and corn, as had been seen by many. . . . A certain man tells that when he lost his member he approached a known witch to ask her to restore it to him. She told him to climb a tree and that he might take which he liked out of a nest in which there were several members. *But when he tried to take a big one, the witch said, "You must not take that one because it belongs to the parish priest."*

Women were tortured to get them to confess. To protect the judges against their seductions they were shaved—both head and crotch—and dragged naked but backward into court so that their eyes could not bewitch anyone.

Among the charges against these accused witches:

They stole the semen of men when they were sleeping. They caused stillbirths and miscarriages. They invaded dreams and caused nocturnal emissions. They were responsible for nymphomania in women and satyriasis in men.

They flew through the air to a place where the devil officiated over a witches' Sabbath. He would kiss their buttocks and filthy parts, and conduct a mockery of Christian ritual. Then he would copulate with all the witches.

(When Henry VIII wanted to get rid of his wife, Anne, he not only had her charged with adultery and incest, but accused her of being a witch. Among the proofs: One of her hands had six fingers.)

From the Middle Ages on it was an accepted canon that the devil often sent an assistant devil to have intercourse with humans—the male incubus for women and the female succubus for men.

The general testimony of the women who were suspected of such intercourse was that it was painful because of the enormous size of his penis, which often was covered with fish scales and the like. And his semen was always ice cold.

A woman accused of witchcraft was often subjected to the ordeal by water. Bound hand and foot she was cast into the water. If she sank she was not a witch; if she floated this was proof that the water had rejected her baptism, which meant that she was a witch.

King James I of England, who disliked women, wrote a book on witchcraft. He assured his readers that the reason there were wens

Water test for witchcraft.

and other disfiguring marks on the bodies of women who were accused of being witches was that "the devil licked them with his tongue, often in some privy parts of their bodies."

Witticisms, Maxims and Epigrams

Love is an affair of credulity.   —OVID

Love is the art of heart and the heart of Art.   —PHILIP BAILEY

We are placed on earth with Nature as our tempter, and then we are blamed for loving and sinning.   —MLLE. LECLERC

A second marriage is the triumph of hope over experience.
                                                        —SAMUEL JOHNSON

They hugged each other very tightly, exchanging kisses rendered surpassingly salty by their tears. This is thought by some to add relish, as with peanuts, by bringing out the sweetness.   —JOHN COLLIER

The greatest happiness in life is the conviction that we are loved, loved for ourselves, or rather loved in spite of ourselves.
—VICTOR HUGO

Let no one think he is loved by anyone when he loves no one.
—EPICTETUS

Come live with me, and be my love,
And we will all the pleasures prove.

—CHRISTOPHER MARLOWE

To be loved, be lovable.   —OVID

There are very few people who are not ashamed of having been in love when they no longer love each other.
—FRANÇOIS LA ROCHEFOUCAULD

I like not only to be loved, but also to be told that I am loved. . . . The realm of silence is large enough beyond the grave. This is the world of light and speech and I shall take leave to tell you that you are very dear.   —GEORGE ELIOT

To love oneself is the beginning of a lifelong romance. —OSCAR WILDE

Of all sexual aberrations, perhaps the most peculiar is chastity.
—REMY DE GOURMONT

Only a man who has loved a woman of genius can appreciate what happiness there is in loving a fool.   —CHARLES MAURICE TALLEYRAND

When the rabbi has marital intercourse the walls shake, and all the Hassidim clap their hands.   —ANONYMOUS

Love ye the stranger, for ye were strangers in the land of Egypt.
—DEUTERONOMY

'Tis better to have loved and lost
Than never to have loved at all.

—ALFRED LORD TENNYSON

Say what you will, 'tis better to be left than never to have been loved.
—WILLIAM CONGREVE

Better to love amiss than nothing to have loved.   —GEORGE CRABBE

Better a positive Wasserman than never to have loved at all.
—GROUCHO MARX

There are many people who would never have been in love if they had
never heard love spoken of.   —FRANÇOIS LA ROCHEFOUCAULD

Love is the business of the idle, but the idleness of the busy.
—HENRY BULWER-LYTTON

In America love is regarded as an infirmity.   —DAVID COHN

Where there's marriage without love there will be love without
marriage.   —BENJAMIN FRANKLIN

To love and win is the best thing; to love and lose, the next best.
—WILLIAM MAKEPEACE THACKERAY

Perhaps they were right in putting love into books. . . . Perhaps it
could not live anywhere else.   —WILLIAM FAULKNER

There is nothing good in love except the physical part.
—COMTE DE BUFFON

Love is the contact of two epidermises.   —SEBASTIAN CHAMFORT

INDEX

186   Index